The Master is more than just kind
O friends, I could never have enough time
to tell you Her boundless Grace.
Only in the remote corner of my heart
I humbly shed tears!

There is none in this world
who's so full of love and Mercy.
It would be my great honour
to be just a swallow;
standing on one leg.
Life after life
singing Her praise!

# Suma Ching Hai
## - A Brief Biographical Sketch

Suma Ching Hai was born in Au Lac. As an adult She made her studies abroad. Later She traveled to many different countries searching for Truth. Eventually, while in seclusion during a sojourn to the Himalayas to practice the Way, She became enlightened. Currently, with infinite compassion, Suma Ching Hai offers the Supreme Method, also known as the Quan Yin Method which She had acquired to those who sincerely believe in and search to practice the Way of Truth.

# CONTENTS

# A LITTLE MESSAGE

*In speaking of God or the Supreme Spirit, we will use a different term of non-sex, to avoid the argument of whether God is a She or a He.*

SHE + HE becomes HES = hes (like in mess).
HER + HIM becomes HIRM = hirm (like in firm).
HERS + HIS becomes HIERS = hiers (like in beers).

*Example: When God wants, Hes makes things happen according to Hiers will to suit Hirm.*

# Master
# Tells
# Stories

# The Story Of The Two Potatoes

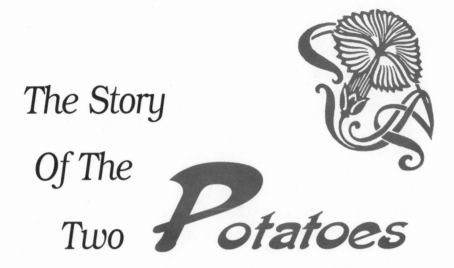

**T**oday I would like to share with you a nice story about how difficult it is to surrender to one's guru, to one's master. It is difficult to be a master. It's more difficult to find a master. Then it's even more difficult to believe, trust, and surrender to this master. The story goes like this.

There was a master who was very prefect, the greatest one, but was not what we'd imagine a "master" to be. Sometimes he'd scold his students. (Laughter) Yes, he might even beat one or two – just like Milarepa, the great Tibetan yogi and his master. This master did all kinds of things that we'd imagine a master should never do. For example, if we came and said, "The master would never get angry," he would get very angry.

We have to be crazy to be a master. (Laughter) If you are normal, you cannot be a master, because in this world everything is opposite, is upside down. What is good, we think is bad.

What is bad, we praise and think is good. Only when you are completely enlightened can you see the funny side of all things in this world. Then you can be crazy, very happily crazy – a very balanced craziness.

One day, this "crazy" master told one of his disciples to take two potatoes and go and eat them. He emphasized again and again that the disciple must eat two potatoes – both of them together. Then he called him again and said, "You must eat two potatoes."

The disciple took two potatoes from the master's hand, went to the street, sat down, and began to eat. Now, it's very easy to eat two potatoes, no? You would think it's not a hard test. Anyone can eat two potatoes. So he was eating and asking himself, "What's the master up to?"

He was thinking like that. But since he had been following his master for a very long time, he knew that whatever the master said, there was a reason and he must obey. So he sat there and ate. Having finished one already, he began to peel the other. Then came a beggar, very hungry, nearly dying, saying, "Please, please give me that potato, because you have eaten one and I've had nothing for many days. I'll die if you don't give it to me!"

Now, what would you do? Should you surrender to your master or to compassion? The master emphasized that he must eat the two potatoes together and the rule is that you never disobey. And the hungry, not to give food to such a hungry person would be very cruel. He sat there, wavering back and forth in his mind between his master and the beggar. But then the beggar was crying, fell down on the ground, and was nearly dying; so the disciple immediately gave the remaining potato to him. Then he went home and the beggar disappeared also.

He went home and reported to his master what had

happened. The master scolded and screamed at the disciple. He was screaming out of sorrow, because he was feeling sorry for the disciple, not because the disciple had dis- obeyed him.

The second potato was blessed with the highest spiritual enlightenment, com- plete enlightenment; while the first potato was blessed with worldly wealth, success and fame. He said, "How stupid you are!" Then he sighed, "Maybe it is your destiny. So poor you couldn't get it!"

After that, the disciple was always successful in the world, gaining a lot of money and fame; but he did not become a master, meaning he never reached the ultimate goal, the highest position in the universe.

This is the problem with most of us. We think we can handle everything and know everything. We think we don't have any ego. We think it is very easy to follow and surrender to a master. No, it isn't easy. Even to eat two potatoes you have a problem. (Laughter)

So, it's hard to dream of doing any other difficult task because we have so many preconceived ideas, we have so many prejudices, social customs and the background education... which have been solidified for many thousands of years. We have been brainwashed with them and it's difficult to wash it out in a short time.

We always think we know all that is right and wrong. What do these prejudices have to do with our enlightenment? They obstruct our way. Whenever the master tells us to do one thing, we do the other thing because we think, "No, no, I know it. My mother told me so, my teacher in school told me this, and my priest in the church has told me that."

We do exactly the opposite of what the master desires us to do, and the master always has to struggle with our prejudice. Most of us are blind, deaf and dumb. Only the master can see clearly. The rest of the people see only in a hazy way or half way, or do not see at all. We think we see, but we don't. We think we understand, but we do not. It is truly great, the illusion of this world. It is truly amazing, the great work of Maya.

It cheats us into believing in anything that we should not believe. We follow it very faithfully, very nicely and obediently until the one who is awakened, enlightened comes along to shake us out of this illusion. But even then, we don't wake up so quickly. Just as in the morning, the alarm clock rings but you say, "Ah...oh...," and it keeps on ringing. Then you turn it off and go back to sleep.

That is why we have so many religions and we have so many so-called paths to liberation. But what do we see? Our world is more and more populated every day. That means, from our world, no one has been liberated – or very few. Otherwise, why hasn't the population decreased? If many had been liberated and gone home – become angels, become God's assistants, God's sons and daughters and lived in paradise forever – then the world would be less populated.

# A Zen Master And The Five Hundred *Flamingos*

Long ago, there was a monk who practiced very well. He had been a monk for many lifetimes, yet he couldn't get liberation from birth and death! You might have become a monk, observed the precepts very strictly, and been very virtuous; but if you cannot get enlightenment, the best you can hope for is to reincarnate and become a monk again. It is actually very good because you might not be able to become a monk even!

This monk reincarnated as a monk many times for five hundred years – a senior monk each time, and he became increasingly virtuous. Though he was not enlightened, he kept the precepts strictly and was very virtuous and honest. The last time he was a monk, wherever he went to beg or lecture, there were always five hundred flamingos that followed him. People were very curious about this phenomenon. Someone who had the ability to see with their heavenly eye said that the flamingos were really his disciples from a previous life. Then, he had five hundred disciples, but he couldn't lead them to liberation because his spiritual power was not strong enough.

His disciples always wanted to go with him whenever he went out – to receive offerings, to attend honorable feasts, or to give lectures. They complained: "Master, you often said that all monastic people are equal! However, each time you go out to enjoy something, you seldom take us along."

The truth was, their master knew that they didn't have sufficient merit to deserve the praise and offerings. Being ordinary human beings, his disciples didn't understand, and they just loved material things. He didn't have any choice, so he took them along when he went out. Later, when the five hundred disciples died, they couldn't reincarnate as monks again but became flamingos instead! Only their master could come back as a monk. So, every time he went out, there were five hundred disciples – now flamingos – with him, just because of their precious master and disciple relationship.

Since he couldn't liberate himself, naturally he couldn't liberate his disciples, who must shoulder the retribution themselves. If your master has tremendous power, he/she can eliminate the minor karmic hindrances that you have incurred. This is why you need an enlightened Master!

# The Monkey-Monk

Long time ago, there was a monk who became a monkey. When the Buddha came into this world to preach the dharma, the Truth, there were many monks who studied under Him. There were some monks who had already attained the fruit of arhatship, but many people did not know that. Other monks sometimes made fun of them because some of them didn't look very good, looked a little bit funny. Like someone called Suma-Tzu, like me.

There was one monk who was very, very naughty. Every time he saw one of the monks running down the hill, he'd say to him, "You look like a monkey running down that hill."

Because he criticized that monk and called him a monkey, for five hundred lifetimes, he had to be born as a monkey.

So take care don't laugh at the monks, because between "monk" and "monkey" the only difference is two letters. Anyhow, if you make fun of an ordinary monk, maybe it's all right. But if that monk has already attained the fruit of arhatship, then you'll be in trouble. You never know which monk has already become arhat, which monk has already attained a very high level of spiritual practice. So you had better take care.

Especially the monks that I send from Miaoli to your country, according to your request to teach you the dharma, you had better take care not to make fun of them, and even not to try to attract them physically. According to Buddhism, if we try to waylay a monk who has been studying under a living Buddha, it is a very terrible sin.

# The *Parrot's* *Advisor*

This is a Jewish story called "The Parrot's Advisor".

There was once a parrot who lived in a palace, an extraordinary parrot of so-called "royal blood". That parrot was gorgeous, most beautiful, probably somewhat resembling "me"! (Laughter) Its master was a princess who loved it very much. They both got along very well, because the parrot was not only beautiful, good looking and elegant, it knew proper etiquette as well. It drank tea like this, which is considered having good manners. It walked with a royal air, with hips swinging side to side, advancing one step and retreating six steps...et cetera. So, this parrot was extremely elegant. Let's call it "Lady Parrot".

Because the parrot belonged to the royal family, it was adorned very beautifully. Even though it was just a parrot as long as it lived in the royal palace, it was a member of the royal family. That parrot could talk and could perhaps even recite the Holy Names. It was very smart, was even fluent in the human language. Its cage was grandly decorated, made of gold and studded with diamonds, pearls, agate, coral... oh, many precious stones!

Every day, the princess sent quite a few so-called attendants to serve this parrot. Each day it lacked nothing. It wore different hats on its head, different pearls on its tail and different rubies on its wings. Various precious stones were woven onto its wings every day. Its whole body shone brightly. Then at meal times, wow, blessed food was delivered to its cage. It did not have to go look for food.

The water that it drank was drawn from the creeks of Yang Ming Mountain, as it was said that the water there tasted better! Furthermore, this water was very soft, very mild for bathing. Therefore, there was an eunuch who went to the Yang Ming Mountain every day to fetch one bottle of water. Occasionally, on the first or the fifteenth day of the month, or on Sundays, for a change of taste, another eunuch would go to Miaoli to collect the water from the Nectar River.

The parrot itself was very colorful! Some of its feathers were green, some were blue, and it was very shiny and bright. It is said that the parrot was very sharp. If Master had not yet blessed the Nectar River water, then it would refuse to drink it. It would demand that the eunuch recite the Holy Names; and only after the eunuch had recited the Holy Names many times, blessing the water from the Nectar River or from Yang Ming Mountain, would it agree to drink it. (Laughter)

Unlike some of you here, who would swallow the food even before offering it to God first. It's okay. If you've already swallowed it, then let it be. There's no need for you to regurgitate it to offer it to God. Just pray to the inner Master to bless the food at the solar plexus. The blessing power works just the same. It would not be blocked by the linings of the stomach. There's no problem. The blessing power can pass through the throat and down into the stomach to bless the already swallowed food.

Oh, now we've come to the second part. I have no word to describe the beauty and the wisdom of the parrot! This parrot knew how to maintain its looks every day so that it was always so beautiful. It didn't become beautiful in one day. Since it was born, only by drinking the Nectar River water, and eating delicious blessed food which had already been blessed by the Holy Names and offered to God, did it grow more and more beautiful each day.

Furthermore, the parrot meditated for two and a half hours every day. It was a pure vegetarian, and would not even eat one insect. In case it swallowed one by mistake, it would regurgitate every single hair of the tiniest caterpillar. It had decided to become a vegetarian when it was young, ever since hearing that all of its ancestors had practiced the Quan Yin Method. The parrot had practiced to such a high level that the princess loved it very much. Maybe its atmosphere was quite good. Its beauty radiated from within.

One day, the princess heard that in a certain country, in some distant place, there was a kind of very rare perfume that she didn't have in her own palace. So, she asked an eunuch to go get it for her. This eunuch was actually the best friend of the parrot because he talked to it every day. Eunuchs in the palace are usually very bored. Since they cannot have girlfriends, what do you think they live for!? Because of that, he usually felt bored; and as it happened that the parrot was there, he talked with it about his private affairs every day. Wow! The two were considered close friends!

The day before the eunuch left, of course, he went to tell the parrot! Although it was a secret mission, he couldn't hold it back from his best friend, and went to say good-bye! Sayonara! Upon hearing that the eunuch was going on such a long trip, of course, it would miss him very much. So the scene of their farewell was kind of touching.

Though that parrot cherished its friendship with the eunuch very much, what did it cherish even more? (A: The princess) "Freedom!" What princess! The princess was the one who tied it down! Why treasure her? Only you would treasure Satan. The world ties you down, yet you treasure it, treasure this life, treasure this body thinking that this body is so great, so beautiful and so strong, et cetera.  This body is what ties our soul here, locks it here.

We concentrate on this body from morning until night, making it beautiful by coloring it red and green, like me.  Then we forget our real Self, forget we are not this body.  Now I have also forgotten my soul because it has run away.  There is only this body left, and whatever it does, doesn't matter.

Thus, it treasured its freedom above all, thinking of flying away day and night.  Even though it was there putting on red and green powder, painting on lipstick and whatever make-up, et cetera, its heart was only thinking of flying away and nothing else.  Of course, it had to eat and had to wear those beautiful clothes; because in the palace, you had to be polite and courteous.  But its mind concentrated on the 'wisdom eye' the whole day long, think-ing only of escaping.

So it told the eunuch, "Ah! We are good friends.  I want to ask a favor of you! Please don't forget."

The eunuch said, "Of course!  I would do anything for you." They were such good friends!

Then it said, "When you are out travelling, if you happen to come across anyone who looks like me, those parrots are my relatives and friends.  You have to tell them that I'm trapped here!  I am suffering greatly, and really not free.  All of the good food here means nothing to me.  Those pearls, precious stones are of no value to me.  Can you ask them if they have any way of rescuing me?"

The eunuch said, "Okay!  I'll try my best.  I will definitely find some parrots and pass the news on to them."

This eunuch, since he also worked in the palace, he didn't

lack anything; but he was also someone else's slave. He understood the value of freedom, thus he understood this parrot very
well! So he decided to help it.

He was gone a long time, looking for the perfume for the
princess. While enjoying the scenery on the way, one day he
came across a large flock of parrots which looked very much like
the princess' parrot in the palace. He then recalled the request of
the parrot in the palace. He went to greet those parrots, and told
them the painful situation of the parrot in the palace.

Among this flock of parrots, there was a master who was
the real master of the parrots. It taught them to practice the Quan
Yin Method. Thus, they went to different places to meditate together every day. On that day, they were on their way to Miaoli
for the big group meditation. Oh! That was in winter, perhaps
they were going to Pingtung! Pingtung is warmer. This real
master was also very clever, with much wisdom! Having practiced
for hundreds of thousands of millions of eons, it looked very magnificent, tranquil, glistening with wisdom, shining with golden
light, and its wisdom eye was wide-opened.

After the so-called real master heard about the painful situation in the palace, it immediately fell over and died, seemingly
dead. It just fell down onto his hand and died, leaving no signs of
vitality, showing no signs of life, dead, absolutely dead, one hundred percent dead. No matter how hard the eunuch shook it, it
couldn't be awakened, really dead. He gave it some water and
opened its mouth, trying to cram something into it; but it did not
eat, completely dead. Not a feather moved and not an eyebrow,
eyelash twitched; it lay there completely "kaputt".

This eunuch was very disappointed, as he hadn't gotten

any advice yet. He didn't get a chance to talk with it before it died. So, he just threw it on the roadside and left. But as he threw it on the roadside, that parrot immediately flew away, tat, tat, tat, tat, la,la,la!.... It flew to Pingtung, joining its companions who had gone ahead for the big group meditation. Uh! That eunuch was shocked! He couldn't understand it! How could that be! He was stunned and stood there puzzled for a long time.

Eventually, he went back to the palace. He couldn't just stand there stunned for the entire day. The parrot in the palace was very happy to see the eunuch. They both held hands and feet, embracing and kissing each other, saying a lot of good things!

"You've lost weight," one would say.

Then the other would say, "You've gained weight."

Those pointless, worldly, astral mannerisms.

That eunuch wanted to tell it many of the interesting things about the trip or some unusual things, but eventually the parrot didn't want to listen. "Those are useless, please don't say anymore! What you ate? What you played? Which karaoke you went to? What dance you did? Which beautiful girl you saw? They are useless, you're an eunuch. Why talk about those beautiful girls!? They're useless as well. Who you danced with is of no concern and of no interest to me! Ayah! No, don't talk about those things!" the parrot said. "Did you meet any of my relatives, my people?"

The eunuch replied, "Yes! Yes! I met a large flock. They seemed to be on their way to group meditation. Each of the parrots had a very big glistening wisdom eye! I was shocked! I respected them a lot. They were very dignified with a look of a lot of blessed merits! Their lower jaws were lowered, their tummies were very big, and their shoulders were very solemn. Flying in the air, they looked like angels..."

Then the parrot grew impatient, "I didn't ask you how they looked! Did they tell you anything? Did they say how I could be liberated?"

Then the eunuch said, "No, no! They seemed not to speak your language. Although their wisdom eyes were opened, their mouths were not; and they could not speak the human language. Thus they did not tell me anything. However, since you've asked, I just remembered something that was very difficult to understand. That is, after I told them your story, there was one who flew onto my hand. Before I could feel happy, it died.

It 'pretended' to be dead, lying there. Then no matter how I shook it, fed it with water and good food, it didn't eat and did not drink. I gave it very fragrant, very rare food, but it did not eat. Very good water from the Nectar River in Miaoli, and it did not care. Didn't eat and didn't drink. It just pretended to be dead.

When I thought that it was dead, I threw it by the roadside. After being tossed away, it immediately flew away very freely and serenely. It even said good-bye to me. Good bye... It spoke quite a few different languages. Originally, I thought it couldn't talk and that it was dead. But it turned out like this. Strange! Until now I still can't figure out what it meant?"

After listening to this, this parrot pretended to be unaffected by it! "Fine! Fine! Thank you very much! I also feel strange. This story is very strange. How could it be so strange!"

Then they both returned to their own homes. The eunuch was busy with his chores and that parrot was busy eating and drinking.

The princess came to see the parrot every morning! The next morning when she came to see the parrot, she saw no parrot in the cage, only a dead body lying there. The princess was very angry and scolded those servants, "You killed it, You killed it."

Anything said was of no use. She ordered them to throw the dead parrot out. When the servant threw it out of the window, at that moment, the eunuch realized the plan of the parrot he had met.

What do you understand? (A: Pretend to be dead.) Pretend to be dead! Right! Then we have to pretend to be dead to this world too. We know the value of the world. We know that the human body is very difficult to obtain. But we do not tell the King of Maya. What is the King of Maya? It is our brain. Don't listen to it. Don't play with it. Don't think that the world is very good to us. If we are dead to the world, then our souls will begin to revive. Thus since ancient times, any real practicing master would tell us to feel dead to the world, meaning we don't cling to anything and don't cling to this world, like being dead. Then we can be free. In fact, if we, from morning till night, feel responsible for people, feel embarrassed, are courteous, then we accompany one another because we are afraid to hurt others' feelings or afraid that others will say we are no good... et cetera. Really, we waste a lot of time!

Today, we accompany this person at his birthday party; tomorrow, we accompany another person at his funeral party; the day after tomorrow, we go to another home accompanying another one at the wedding party; then the day after, we go to be a witness in the court room for their divorce; because we are kind, courteous, et cetera. Then how could we have the time?

Today we receive this person's talkative telephone call, then the day after we answer to another person's senseless conversation. Also there is newspaper-reading, television-watching – at least watching the news, knowing who killed whom. Then the next day what? If we have a lot of relatives, we would really be busy to death. Thus, to be able to find time to practice in this world is very difficult indeed! If we are tied down like this, basically we are not able to get out. If we do not pretend to be dead, would there be any other way? No!

What is pretending to be dead? We pretend to be deaf and dumb. Let them misunderstand, let them scold us, it does not matter. We still have to have a boundary, knowing what is the priority. Whatever we can do, we do. The other things we can not do, we have to let them be. We have to pretend to be dead – pretending not to know the courtesy, pretending not to know today is his birthday, pretending not to know tomorrow is his funeral.

If our time permits, if it is possible with our lives, of course, we can have any kind of courtesy! If our lives are already so busy, and we are tied down so much, we have to find ways to untie some of the knots, at least to free both our hands; or else if we're all tied up, how to move? We can not pretend to be dead one hundred percent, but we could pretend eighty percent. Eighty percent is quite free already.

Like the parrot, if it didn't pretend to be completely dead, it could pretend eighty percent. Pretending to be ill is okay too. They would definitely take it out to see the doctor. Then it could think of ways to fly away. But that would be more risky. Pretending to be completely dead is better. People would throw it away. After that, it would fly away.

It is the same with us practitioners. We lack nothing in this world, but in fact, we also don't feel free. What we are longing most for is our liberation. What is 'liberation'? Oh! We wouldn't have any desires, no greed! Our lives would be tranquil, contented. Our insides would be very happy. On the outside, we'd be able to take care of our situations. Then we would have been liberated in this life.

When we really die, since we are liberated in this life, then in the next life we would also be liberated. Because we don't cling to the world when we are alive, then when we die, how could we cling to anything? Like the parrot, it had all the good food in the cage, yet it didn't want to eat. How could it cling to it after it was able to fly and had its own freedom? Thus, practitioners are like this parrot!

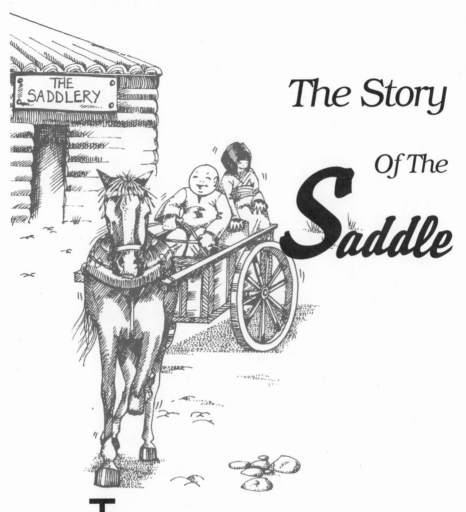

THE SADDLERY

# The Story

## Of The

# Saddle

This is a story of the saddle. Originally, there were no saddles for horses. It was later, perhaps derived from the benefit of some spiritual practice, that saddles were invented.

There was a man named Liao Hu. Unlike us, being kind, he was a very, very mean and very, very vicious government official. He died when he was sixty-two years old and went to see the King of Hell. This King of Hell was from Formosa and was somewhat peculiar; he was black on the left side and white on the right. I wonder why? (Laughter)

The King of Hell flipped through the book of sins and merits to see what good and bad deeds this man had done before his death. He found out that this man had created so much bad karma, and had never given to any charity. He had never been to Hong Kong to protest on behalf of the refugees. (Laughter) He had never given any offerings to the temples and had never been in a church. He had never given money to the beggars and never donated a penny to Tse-Chi Charity or any other charitable organizations.

Liao Hu was not a vegetarian, he didn't eat meat because he was very stingy. It wasn't because he wanted to become a Buddha that he didn't eat meat. Therefore, I have told you that being a vegetarian won't make you a Buddha; it depends on your purpose. This man didn't eat meat because he didn't want to spend money to buy meat for the rest of the family. Sometimes when he craved it, he would hide in the bathroom and eat a piece of meat all by himself. Then he'd come out after he had finished eating so his family wouldn't know. This is how bad he was.

He had never attended Suma Ching Hai's lectures. (Laughter) So the King of Hell looked around and couldn't find anything to save him; there was only bad karma, no merit at all. Once, a disciple of Suma Ching Hai tried to give him a sample booklet; it was free. But he refused because he said the booklet would take up space in his plastic bag for groceries. (Laughter) How could anyone possibly save him?!

So the King of Hell said, "No Good! Forget it! Forget it! I have tried my best to search every corner of the book, but it is full of bad karma. Now you have to be born as a horse to pay for your past bad deeds."

So saying, he made a hand mudra and a foot mudra, and gave him a kick. Thus he fell and was born as a horse. This horse had its name on an ID card. That was how it was known that it was the reincarnation of Liao Hu.

This horse named Liao Hu grew bigger and bigger. It ate a lot of grass and was very satisfied. In its past life, it didn't want to buy meat, not even tofu, so eating grass was all it had; and it was quite contented. It never complained about eating grass; besides, it was all free! Even being a horse, it was still very stingy. It would eat the cheap, rotting grass, and save the fresh grass to sell to the other horses. (Laughter)

When it grew up, its master put it to work. It had to carry firewood, cooking oil, rice and other necessities home. Sometimes, it had to pull a wagon with forty or fifty fat people on it. Oh! It couldn't bear it; but if it didn't keep walking, the horseman would whip it. It hated the whole situation and couldn't take it anymore. The horseman was mean to it also. He would kick it, whip it, and treat it cruelly. When he rode the horse, there was no saddle, so it was quite uncomfortable and even painful for the horse. This horse had just been reincarnated from a human being. It still carried the temperament of a human instead of a horse. So it was very annoyed, very sad and finally went on a hunger strike. It quit eating for three or four days and then died. Some of the disciples of Suma Ching Hai took pity on it, and recited sutras, sang Hallelujah, and prayed for it. But even then, its karma was still too heavy, so it went down to see the King of Hell.

The King of Hell was angry and kept yelling at him, "Are you trying to escape your bad karma? Can you? No, you cannot! I'm telling you, if I want you to be a horse, then you'll be a horse; if I want you to be a dog, then you'll be a dog. You cannot escape in such a way. Don't you know that until you have fully paid for your bad deeds you cannot run away?"

The King of Hell scolded him until his own face was red-hot. "You cheated me! Your time was not up yet, your karma had not been paid in full, and now you went and starved yourself to death on purpose. This is cheating!"

So now the King of Hell made him into a dog. He waved at him from head to toe and gave him a kick. Thus he fell into the womb of a mother dog and was born.

Even though he was a dog now, Liao Hu still had some human qualities and intelligence. He was feeling very sad, very annoyed, very miserable, very worried, very depressed, very help-less, very powerless and very bored (which in Chinese sounds similar to his name Hu, Liao). (Master and everyone laugh.) But he dared not commit suicide again, knowing that the King of Hell would punish him even more.

He sat there and thought, "I cannot starve myself now! Even though this dog food is really unappetizing, I have to eat it. Otherwise, I don't know how the King of Hell will punish me!"

He thought and thought using his own dog thinking. Then, oh, suddenly he was enlightened! He said, "Now if I bite my master hard, he will kill me. Ha! (Master and everyone laugh.) Then I would die without having committed suicide!"

He got started right away. He recited some sutras, "Da, da, da, da...." in order to liberate himself while he waited for his master to return. After smoking and drinking, his master came back. The dog wagged its tail then bit the master's behind and front. It was so painful and he was drunk and angry, so he picked up a big bat to hit it. The dog was kaput!

He went to the Kingdom of Hell again. The King of Hell was mad and of course, scolded it severely again. "You bad dog! How dare you cheat me again! Now, hmm, you'll get fifty lashes first."

After the beating, he was to be born as a snake. Gosh! Being a dog wasn't that bad, but to be a snake is really troublesome. The more he tried to escape, the worse it got.

As a snake, the King of Hell threw him in a dungeon and locked him up so he had nowhere to go. Nevertheless, he was able to dig a hole and slip away. Now he dared not commit suicide or bite others, knowing that would only make him more guilty. So, mm, he thought and thought with his snake brain, and finally decided to crawl into the middle of the road to lie down and sleep. (Master and everyone laugh.) That person was full of ideas – sleeping in the middle of the road at night! In ancient times, there were no street lights. So when a car went by, he was chopped into a few pieces and liberated!

Looking at the pitiful sight, the King of Hell decided he had had enough punishment. Finally, he was victorious! The King of

Hell felt sorry for his suffering and misery, and couldn't bear to punish him anymore. Ah! The King of Hell was quite compassionate after all! He must have practiced the Quan Yin Method. Half way only, that's why he was half white (laughter) and half black! So he was forgiven and was allowed to be born as a human being.

Once again, he was to be a government official. But he was reminded to be virtuous and to govern his people wisely and kindly. He must not be greedy or corrupt; he must not be vicious or mistreat people. "Otherwise," the King of Hell warned him, "I will not forgive you! You must also keep the five precepts."

He even told him to go find Suma Ching Hai to get initiation! (Applause.) Just kidding! These kind of people are very hard to save. It's better he doesn't come to us! (Master laughs.)

However, he really looked Her up! She taught him to keep the five precepts, be a vegetarian, meditate two and half hours every day, attend group meditations, speak up or protest for others in suffering... et cetera. From that day on, he became a very good person; and later, a very virtuous government official. He would instruct his subordinates to use saddles when they rode the horses, not to kick the horses with their heels, and not to whip them too hard, as he remembered how much he had suffered when he was a horse. He was also very generous and gentle with his people. Therefore, later all his bad karma was erased.

# Dangers Of Magical Power Without Wisdom

**T**here is another story about some eager students who went to study with a master. Because the master had a lot of magical powers, they also wanted to have some. However, the master always refused and refused, telling them that they were not ready for anything like that. It is very dangerous to have spiritual powers without virtue and wisdom. But the students didn't want to listen to all this. They saw the master doing all kinds of miraculous performances, and they wanted to have some. Especially the one that raised the dead back to life again, they loved to play that. So, they kept pressing the master all the time until one day the master gave in and taught them the secret formula for raising the dead back to life.

With this new discovery, they were very happy. So they just left the master, because they thought that was all they wanted. They went together somewhere else. During the journey, they went through some very desolated places. For many hundreds of

years no one had lived there. There were some bones on the road; they wanted to test the power of their newly learned skill. They did the mantra, hand gesture and foot gesture, bla, bla, bla like this. Suddenly all the bones flew

into the air, stuck together, and formed the original appearance of a live animal. All the flesh came back to life, then the horns, then the fangs

also grew out again. It became a dinosaur from many millions of years ago. It was so huge. It chased and ate them, liberated them.

That is also one of the dangers of being a copycat.

Copying the master without having the wisdom of a real enlightened person, without having the power to control our curiosity, without having the compassion to do the things in the right moment just when sentient beings need you to help and not because of your curiosity or because you want to show off your power, is very dangerous. That is why in our spiritual practice, we do not encourage people to use magical power. If you have any, you had better not use it.

As I have told you already, it is some kind of borrowed substance from the universal powerhouse, and it is not a higher powerhouse. Whatever you borrow from a lower existence, you must pay back with interest. If you have it from the most high, from the natural circulation of supreme wisdom and power, then it belongs to you, to the God power; and you don't have to pay back.

There was one master, I don't know the name. He was getting older and older. Then of course, his eyes became blurred with age, so much that he could not see the disciples and could not recognize the surroundings anymore. One psychic healer... (sometimes they put their hands on you and they can heal you, things like that) said to the master, "You come to me, entrust yourself to me, I can heal your eyes, make you see again."

But the master said, "No, no. I see what I need to see already, inside. Other things don't matter so much."

That is the right attitude for any spiritual practitioner. For us, we should never feel greedy for magical healing, magical power and all these kinds of convenient things. They are temporary, only offer a little relief and in turn, we lose a lot of things. There is nothing within the three worlds that we can get for free. Only on the fifth plane is everything in abundance and no charge. Everything else is made from material substances, in this world and within the three worlds. If we take too much for ourselves, then there will be a shortage somewhere else. Therefore magical power is nothing but to take something from somewhere else and bring it to another place.

# Too Greedy

**H**ere is an Au Lac story. A long time ago, there was a very poor family. When the parents died, they left some farm properties to their two sons. The elder brother was smarter, more conniving, and knew more about worldly schemes. The younger brother was not very sensible, but he was kinder, purer and had faith. After their parents passed away, they started to divide up the properties.

The elder brother was married, while the younger one was not. The elder brother said to the younger one, "It's better to let me take care of these properties. Since you have no wife, no children and you don't know how to take care of these properties, it would be useless to give them to you. However, since I know that you're a very good brother, I'll let you have a starfruit tree. The starfruit tree in that corner is yours and the rest of the properties are all mine. Okay?" The younger brother said, "Okay." (Audience laughs.) Then, every day the elder brother worked on the farm. He

32

became prosperous and lived well. The younger brother also lived well on his starfruit tree. When the starfruit were ripe, he picked them and sold them. The tree was quite big and bore much fruit. If he couldn't sell all of them, he would take the remaining back to make starfruit juice and preserved starfruit. He was quite resourceful. He preserved some in sugar, some in salt and some in vinegar. He produced many kinds of starfruit products, which became very, very famous. Many people liked them and came from faraway places to buy them. So he earned enough money for himself and lived comfortably and contentedly. He wasn't very rich, but he was easily satisfied.

One day, he went out to buy some things for making preserved starfruit. When he came back home, he saw that almost half of the fruit had been eaten up. He felt very sad. Then he saw a crow still on the tree, continuing to eat his starfruit. "Oh!" he thought. "How can it be?" So he asked the crow, "Why are you eating my starfruit?"

The crow said, "I'm hungry!" (Audience laughs.)

It was very simple. The crow ate because it was hungry.

"When you're hungry, don't you eat?" asked the crow.

He said, "Of course I eat."

"Then why did you ask me?"

The younger brother was dumb and didn't know how to argue, so he was a little dazed. He thought, "Of course, when the crow is hungry, it eats. Why did I ask? (Master and audience laugh.) However, this tree is all I have. If it's eaten up, I'll be finished, I'll starve tomorrow and have no food to eat."

Then he told the crow what he felt.

This crow was a strange crow; it didn't look like an ordinary one. Its beak was very long. (Audience laughs.) A crow doesn't have ears, but this crow had big ears with an earring hanging there. (Master and audience laugh.) Its feathers were curly and very fashionable. Its clothes were quite beautiful. Although it was a crow, its clothes were of all colors.

The younger brother said to the crow, "It's not that I begrudge you the starfruit. Of course, you can eat them when you're hungry. You're welcome. However, frankly speaking, after my parents passed away, my brother left only this tree for me. I have to rely on it to live. I'm dumb and I can't do other things. I would die without this tree. This is my pitiful situation. It's not that I begrudge you the starfruit."

Upon hearing this, the crow was touched and said, "Well! You're such a nice person. All right, all right. It's no problem. Since I've eaten your starfruit, I'll repay you with gold. Is that all right?"

Then the younger brother said, "All right!" (Master and audience laugh.)

He could only say "okay" or "all right," nothing else. He wouldn't refuse people.

So the crow said to him, "Tomorrow, early morning at three o'clock, I'll come here to pick you up. Now you go home and find a piece of cloth to sew a bag this big, this long and this wide. Tomorrow I'll take you to get pearls, jewels and gold."

"Okay!" The younger brother went home and made a bag this big, this long and this wide – no more and no less.

The next morning, as expected, the crow was waiting there for him. The crow said, "All right. Now you get on my back. I'll fly you across the sea. While flying, you can't speak and can't open your eyes. No matter what happens, you shouldn't disobey my order, or you won't survive."

The younger brother said, "Okay!"

After he got on the crow's back and held its neck, it flew.

Suddenly
the crow
became
very big.
The younger
brother felt com-
fortable sitting on it
and fell asleep. He could
do Quan Yin there, no
problem. (Audience laughs.)
No, he couldn't do Quan Yin, he
could do Quan Guang only.

We spiritual practitioners don't speak if we aren't asked. Besides "okay" and "all right," we shouldn't say anything else. The Bible also says the same thing: When asked, you should only say "okay" and "all right". You shouldn't talk nonsense. This means that we should conserve our speech and not talk.

This younger brother practiced the Quan Yin Method and was very good. When he was told not to speak, he didn't speak. Shortly after he started to meditate, he went into samadhi. Then they arrived at the place.

Oh! That place had beautiful mountains, beautiful beaches and all kinds of things. Pearls and jewels were piled into a huge mountain. Trees and everything were made of pearls and jewels.

35

The leaves were all of gold and the branches were made of pearls and jewels. Everything was from pearls and jewels. There were no stones, only pearls and jewels everywhere.

Then the crow told him, "Now you pick all your favorite pearls and jewels and put them in your bag. Then we'll go home immediately."

The younger brother said, "Okay!"

He put his favorite and the most precious things in his bag, hung the bag on his belt, and jumped on the crow. As the crow flew him back, he closed his eyes and meditated again. He entered samadhi, then they were home.

From that day on, the younger brother was rich. He sold the pearls and jewels, built another house, married a beautiful girl, and then raised a beautiful kitten. (Audience laughs.) He lived a very comfortable life.

A long time afterwards, upon hearing that the younger brother suddenly became very rich, the elder brother came from a very faraway place to visit him. The elder brother asked the younger one how he suddenly became so rich.

The younger one said, "Well! It was thanks to you and your merit. It was all due to your blessings. I became rich because you gave me the starfruit tree. Thank you, brother!"

Then he prostrated to his elder brother.

The elder brother asked, "How did the starfruit tree make you rich?"

Of course the younger brother told him everything.

Well, the elder brother's desire was aroused, "Oh! It was certainly my merit. All right, now you can move to my place to live. The properties are all yours. This starfruit tree is mine. (Master and audience laugh.) We'll exchange now. You've had the starfruit tree for too long. I was going to exchange with you, because we should take care of our parents' properties in turn.

I've taken care of them for many years and become weary. Now it's your turn. You go back there. Now I'll take care of the starfruit tree. Okay?"

The younger brother said, "Okay!"

He then moved to his elder brother's place.

The elder brother set up a hammock and waited under the starfruit tree every day. As expected, one day, a crow came and ate the starfruit. The elder brother pretended to be annoyed and said, "If you eat my starfruit, I'll starve to death." He then "Da, da, da...," imitating his brother's tone.

Then the crow said, "No problem. Since I've eaten your starfruit, I'll repay you with gold. Okay?"

The elder brother said, "Okay!"

The crow then said, "Wait here for me tomorrow morning at three o'clock. You should sew a bag of this length and this width. Then I'll take you to pick pearls, jewels and gold."

The elder brother immediately went home and cut some cloth. However, what he cut was as big as a Quan Yin shawl. (Master and audience laugh.) It was this long and this wide. He put two pieces together and that was it; he made full use of it. (Audience laughs.) He sewed a bag this big.

Ah! He went there to wait at two o'clock in the morning. However, the crow wouldn't come early. It was on time. At three o'clock, it came to pick the elder brother up. So the elder brother got on its back. He was told to hold onto its neck, not to speak and not to open his eyes.

Well! The elder brother was very bad. He didn't practice the Quan Yin Method and wasn't a vegetarian, so his karma was heavy. The crow could hardly fly across the sea. The crow used special magical powers and made it over. The elder brother heard "Hu! Hu! Hu!" and felt the wind blowing strongly. After flying for a long time, he almost asked, "Have we arrived there yet?" (Master laughs.) Fortunately, the crow slapped him with its wing then he knew; he remembered and didn't ask anymore.

Finally, they got there. Well! It seemed to be a very long journey. It was long for the crow as well as for the elder brother. Both of them were exhausted. After the crow put him down, it immediately went to take a nap. "You go pick your favorite pearls and jewels. I have to take a nap before I can take you back. What have you been eating to make you so heavy? Were you born in the year of the elephant?" (Laughter)

We were all born in the year of the horse or the rat, but he was born in the year of the elephant. Maybe his karma was heavier. (Laughter) After the crow took a nap, the elder brother still hadn't finished picking his pearls and jewels. Whatever he saw made his eyes light up. He wanted everything. He couldn't part with this or that. He kept selecting. After a long time, he still hadn't finished.

Finally, the crow woke up and said, "You can't do this anymore. Just take anything. Time is up. We can't stay here any longer. If we stay here, we won't be able to get home. Quickly get on my back."

At that time, he quickly put everything in his bag. Well! It was very, very difficult for him to get on the crow's back. The crow said, "No, it's too heavy. You should take some out, or I won't be able to fly."

The elder brother was greedy, he took only one pearl out and threw it down.

The crow said, "No, no. It's not enough. Take out some more."

So he took out another pearl this big and threw it down.

"Well!" the crow said. "No! If you don't take out more, we can't fly. I can't fly up now."

The elder brother truly couldn't part with them, but he threw down a handful anyway. Then the crow said, "We can't stay anymore. We have to leave. Time is up."

It took the crow a great deal of effort to fly up. On their way, there was the sea beneath them and nothing else in sight. A typhoon came and it was strong; the crow's wings were not balanced. It tried its best to stay balanced; however, the wind was too strong and the crow swayed and became unstable.

Then the elder brother said, "If you fly like this, I'll die. What are you doing?" Then he opened his eyes, "Wow! The sea!"

Since he opened his mouth and eyes the pearls and jewels slipped from his hands. The elder brother and his pearls and jewels fell down together.

He was told to make the bag this long and this wide, but as a result of making it too big, of course, the crow couldn't bear the weight. We human beings are similar to the elder bother. We're too greedy, so somethimes we end up with nothing.

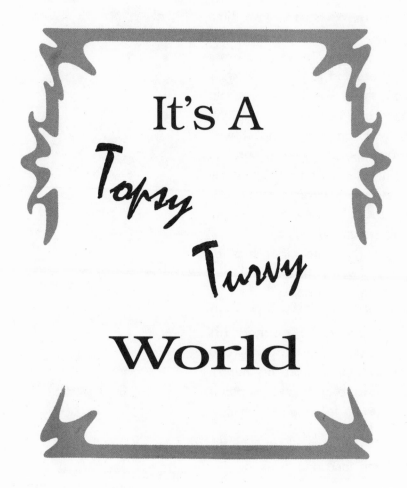

It's A
Topsy
Turvy
World

# T

here was a great enlightened master and he had a disciple. The disciple had followed him for only a short time. The enlightened master had already attained the Truth, and he often travelled around the world to liberate any person with whom he had affinity. The disciple followed him everywhere. This master was so pure and upright that he was reluctant to even beg. Therefore, he always hid himself, and walked on the concealed mountain paths. On the way, he just randomly picked some fruit or wild vegetables to eat; he ate whatever was available. In this way, and after a long time, of course the disciple couldn't stand it anymore!

One day, the disciple went into town alone, hoping to find a wealthy household from which to beg. Eventually, he came to a household where many people were rejoicing and having a feast. Everyone could go in and eat the food. Extremely delighted, he went in and filled himself to the full. He also took some back for his master. Since the disciple had brought the food, the master ate it. While eating, the master laughed and said, "It is a foe and creditor coming back to claim and pay a debt. There is nothing to rejoice at!"

The disciple was perplexed by these words and didn't understand what his master meant. A baby has just been born to that family. They are overjoyed and have invited everyone to the feast. They are so happy, yet master said that it is their foe and creditor coming because of a debt. He thought, "Perhaps master has eaten too many sour fruit, so his mind is not very normal." (Master laughs.)

He didn't say anything, though he still had some faith in the master, so he didn't leave.

That family had prayed many years for a child. Now that they were given a son, they planned to celebrate continuously for many days. The next day, the disciple again went to beg for food. Since this household was entertaining guests free of charge, it would be a great pity if one did not go to enjoy it! In a delightful mood, he hoped to enjoy the food again.

Unexpectedly, before he entered the door, he saw everyone running around in confusion and crying noisily. There was no food at all. Yesterday, the parents of the child were very happy, but today they were lying on the floor blaming God. It happened that the child who was born yesterday had just died.

Having had nothing to eat, he wandered around to see whether there was anything left over. People were preparing for the funeral, so there was nothing to eat. Therefore, he just quickly snatched something and ran away! No one paid any attention to him. He went back and told his master, "Master, something has gone wrong! The child who was born yesterday is dead now.

There is no good food today, so I just brought you something left over from yesterday."

The master then laughed loudly. The disciple asked him, "What are you laughing at? Their child is dead and they are so sad. Why are you laughing?"

The master said, "The world is topsy-turvy! The foe came yesterday, then they were happy. Today the foe has gone, then they are sad!"

The disciple questioned the reasoning of this statement, and his master explained, "Originally, that child was the neighbor of this family. He lent some money to them before, which they never repaid. Later, when they became rich, they forgot the debt. After their neighbor died, he reincarnated as their child, hoping to consume their entire wealth. Because of the birth of the child, they entertained many guests and spent all the money. The amount that he wanted to reclaim was spent in one day, so he had no reason to stay any longer. He left after the debt had been paid." (Applause)

We human beings experience delight, anger, sorrow and happiness, all because of ignorance. We don't know why we are delighted, why we are angry, why we are sad, and why we are happy. It is very difficult for us to judge who is our relative or friend, and who is our foe. Unless we pursue spiritual practice, we have no way to find out.

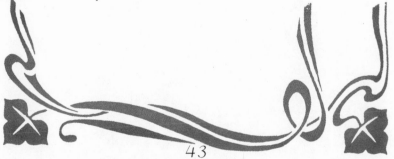

# The Apprenticeship
# *Of* Moses

## Silence And
## Acceptance

You know Moses? Everyone knows. Now, Moses was the great man of the Ten Commandments. He was supposed to have been in connection with God. He was supposed to have known God. He was supposed to have heard God, and then he was supposed to have gotten the Commandments directly from God. But then, even though they were God's Commandments, in between, they were broken, changed many times. I wonder why? Perhaps, it was not God's temper, (Master laughs) it was Moses'. Like my temper, his was very big. (Master laughs.)

He was very angry, and he threw the stone tablets which contained the Ten Commandments from God. I think later he made them again. Probably took him another forty days (Master laughs) to carve the stones into letters. Takes a long time.

So now let's see what else Moses did during his lifetime. This is a short story about Moses when he was still in apprenticeship of masterhood. He was not yet a master, so his temper didn't have time to flare up yet. But still you can see something here. Moses was supposed to have been a master later on. So before he led the people from the land of Egypt, he apprenticed with a great master.

The first discipline that this master imposed on Moses was that of silence. The two of them wandered through the countryside one day, so the master imposed the discipline of silence upon him. The master probably accepted Moses as his disciple, and probably had seen that he was a potential master for the future.

But nevertheless, as you know, to teach anyone is very "easy". (Master laughs.) But to make him believe, understand, and uphold your teachings is very difficult. It's okay you can teach, but if he listens or not, that's another matter. And that

45

matter is very important, crucial and very, very difficult. So Moses began his apprenticeship with the master, and the master told him to keep silence whatever happens. Keep silence means keep your mouth... shut. But it's very difficult.

Then, the master said, "Doesn't matter what happens, you have to keep silence. Don't talk at all until I allow you to."

Moses said, "D'accord (French). Okay."

Then the two of them wandered through the countryside for many days, sometimes stopping here, sometimes stopping there – stopped in a hotel. One day they passed by very, very beautiful countryside. The beauty of it was so extraordinary and dazzling that Moses couldn't help but open his eyes to look, and then opened his mouth as well. He didn't open it alone, he made some sound out of it, "Oh! Master, isn't that beautiful?" (Master and audience laugh.)

But the master forgave him. "I told you to keep your mouth s-h-u-t, shut." (Audience laughs.)

Moses said, "Oh, oh, forgive me, master. Forgive. Forgive. I will shut up. I will not talk again."

When they went further down the road, they came across a river. There was a mother crying on the bank of the river because her baby happened to have been swept away by the current. The current was very, very strong. Moses wanted to save the child and the master did not let him. Of course Moses also could not do it because the current was very strong.

He said to the master, "Master, you are powerful. You're almighty. Can you save the baby? How can you keep silent and just stand here!? The mother is crying. You don't see? The child is drowning, and you keep silent!"

The master said, "Sh! Silence!"

He also gave him a good look like this. (Master displays a serious, rigid gaze. Audience laughs.) You know that look very well, from someone I would not mention the name. (Audience laughs.) When She is angry, She looks like that too. Her eyes become twice bigger than usual. (Audience laughs.) Now, you know that person. Someone called something Tzu, Tzu, Tzu – I don't know that person.

Even though Moses obeyed the master and kept his mouth shut, after the baby drowning incident, he was very, very troubled in his heart. But he could not ask anything. He kept criticizing the master all the time. He said, "This must be a very insensitive man; has no compassion, no love for humankind. He preaches all the time that we must be com-

passionate; we must have love for humankind; we must help the needy, the troubled, the ones in danger and all that; we must help humankind. And here he was standing around, watching the baby drowning, the mother helplessly crying, and he did nothing."

He was having doubt in his heart – very, very much doubt and very, very much troubled; a lot of critical thoughts about the master, but he just kept his mouth shut. Even though Moses begged him for magical power and things like that, the master did not help. He knew it was not correct to criticize the master, but he couldn't help it; and he couldn't dispel all this negative thinking about the master for a long period of time.

Then, during the course of their wandering around the country, perhaps they went around to see other disciples. Before they didn't have cars like today, so probably they had to go on foot. Sometimes they could go on horse carts, if they had money. Perhaps the two didn't have that much, so they wandered around on foot.

One day, they came to the seashore. They both saw a boat sinking with the whole crew members. So Moses' big mouth could not help to open again. He said, "Look, master! The whole boat is sinking. Did you see that? And the whole crew members are sinking. Can you do something about it?"

The master said, "Sh-sh-sh! Keep silence."

That's all he said. Moses, of course, didn't say anything else and kept silent. But his criticizing thoughts kept increasing and increasing many fold. Very troubled was his heart – very, very heavy and troubled.

When he got back home, he complained – not to the master but to God. He said, "God! You told me to follow this guy, but You don't know what kind of guy he is." (Master and everyone laugh.)

God said, "Don't talk nonsense! How do I not know?"

Moses talked to Hirm like that and continued to say, "But You don't know, God. He saw a child dying and he saw a ship sinking with the whole crew members – thirty-odd people on it all dying, and he didn't do anything. Not even move his heart or blink his eyes. That's the person that guy is. And, You told me to follow him."

So God said to him, "It's you who don't know. The child who drowned was a person who was meant to bring a very great war between two nations, in which many hundreds of thousands of people would have died and millions wounded. So it was good that the disaster had befallen him, and that he drowned – saved a lot of people's lives. For that sinking ship, that was a ship of pirates. The pirates were supposed to go and make a very big plunder near the seashore port, very near to where they sank. It was good that the ship sank and all the pirates died. It saved the people of that town from being robbed, killed, raped, and all kinds of bad things done to them by these pirates. Now you know that all the innocent people were saved by the incidence of a baby drowning and the sinking pirate ship."

Of course, Moses kept his mouth shut – finally, (Master and audience laugh) and his "inside mouth" shut too. That is important. Not that because outside he doesn't speak, inside he is quiet.

So you see, Moses was supposed to be a future master of some kind at least. And during the disciple apprenticeship, he was such a difficult and ignorant student. Can you imagine how much harder it is for any master to teach ordinary humankind with lesser intelligence, lesser wisdom and lesser merit? Because to be a master, he must be a very great person – a lot of merit and a lot of wisdom already. Very high-level person. Now to teach such a high-level person, the master must go through a lot of hardship like this.

You just think if Moses obeys him and keeps silence, that's good enough? No, it's not. It's not what he does outside, it's what is inside that will project some kind of harmful energy, and sometimes very discomforting energy to the master. Even though the master keeps silent and bears it all, it doesn't mean that it doesn't hurt. It might not hurt the body of the master, but it might hurt the mental or the energy field of the master. Not the wisdom of the master, not the compassion and the love, and not the real person of the master; but it hurts his mental ability, maybe. Maybe it hurts even his body. If something is too great a burden for the mental ability to bear, then it will come out and affect the body as well.

So mental and physical both would be affected, if the energy is so strong and so negative. Mostly, when the disciple is so close, such as Moses to his master, then this energy would affect him very, very strongly and directly; and it would be very unbearable. But the master, of course, would keep silence and wouldn't talk about it since there was no evidence because Moses kept silent. No one would know that he was attacking the master with his mental projection, which is just as hard-hitting as any physical beating outside. Believe me.

# The *Bird* That Saved The Forest

Now I want to tell you a story for little kids! It's about one of Shakyamuni Buddha's previous lives. There are a lot of stories of His previous lives, and this is about Him being a parrot.

Once Shakyamuni Buddha reincarnated as a tiny parrot. This parrot lived in a small forest. It lived very happily without a worry in the world. Besides meditating two hours a day, it just flew around the clouds and trees, singing and dancing. All the animals in the forest liked it very much, so it went around visiting friends. They all carried "ID cards". (Master laughs.) No one was a stranger around there. So no matter where it went, it greeted everyone saying "Hello!" Because it thought that God had given it the ability to fly, it felt really lucky and happy!

One day, the sky suddenly clouded and the world became very very dark. Then a bright flash of lightning came! The lightning hit a dry dead tree. Around the tree was a lot of dry grass, so a fire started. The wind blew the fire around. Immediately, the whole forest was on fire. The animals ran all around looking for places to hide. Terrible! But they didn't know where to go because they lived right in the middle of the forest and there was no where to go! No matter where they went  they saw fire coming towards them. They were trapped in an ocean of fire. They were in pain! Some could not breathe anymore – everywhere was smoke and there wasn't enough oxygen!

This tiny parrot, previously Shakyamuni Buddha, just flew around and around. It flew into the fire and smoke, and kept on yelling with a microphone: " Run quickly! There's a fire! Go there! There's no fire there, quickly!"

But the forest was too big, and the parrot too tiny to be heard. There was a loud noise of wind and fire all around, so its tiny voice was lost in the fire and wind. Many animals got burned, and choked to death in pain. It still kept on yelling: "Go quickly to the river!"

But a lot of animals could not run there.

During the emergency situation, it had the idea of using water to put out the fire. So it flew to the river, soaked itself with water, flew back, and dripped the water down onto the forest. Even though it knew it wasn't enough, it kept doing that again and again. It continued to think: "I'm doing my best."

So it sacrificed itself, flying back and forth to the river to soak itself up with water and fly back to the forest to drip down a few drops of water. It wasn't any use, but it still did it, again and again, until it turned all black and greasy. Its body was covered with ash. It looked like a crow rather then a parrot. It kept on doing it, even though it was very tired. Then it said to itself: "I am just a little bird. What can I do at a time like this? At least I can do the best I can. I will fly as long as I can."

At that time, the gods and angels in heaven were sitting up there sipping nectar wine. They were sitting on their golden thrones in their beautiful, shiny palace. There was light all over so there was no need for electricity. They were eating and drinking happily, (Master

53

laughs) eating heavenly delicacies, and drinking that sweet nectar wine. They were kind of drunk, but very happy.

Suddenly they looked down into the forest because they saw smoke coming up from there. They looked down and saw this little tiny black spot, flying around and around the forest and the river. It was difficult to recognize what kind of bird it was. They saw it soak itself in the water then fly back to drop water on the raging forest fire.

One or two of them, with large mouths eating blessed food, said: "Ha! Do you see that stupid, little bird? Its brain is out of order! (Master and everyone laugh.) How is it possible that it could put out the huge forest fire with just a few drops of water from its wings? Incredibly stupid! Of course, it's just a bird!"

They just laughed at it up there while watching it. They thought it was funny. But one of the gods in the group saw what was happening and was touched. So he transformed himself into a big bird. The huge bird flew down to where that tiny parrot was! The tiny parrot was still flying back and forth, fluttering its wings to drop water down onto the forest.

All of a sudden, the parrot saw this huge bird. It never saw such a beautiful bird before. Its wings were the colors of the rainbow! Its eyes were as big and shiny as a steel cup. Its whole body glowed with the elegant power of love. The parrot all of a sudden felt very comfortable! But it still didn't forget its duty; it kept on fluttering its wings and dropping water down. Even though it was very tired, it still went down into the river and soaked itself in it.

The huge bird flew after it, saying: "Hey little parrot, don't be stupid! Go take some rest! Don't go into that burning forest! You have to wake up before it's too late or else you'll just die in there!"

The parrot wouldn't listen. It said: "I don't have time. I don't have time even to listen to you! I have an important task in my hands! I have to do my duty. I'll do as much as my weak body can do! I don't have time to listen to you!"

So it kept on flying back and forth to the river and the forest. It still wanted to put out the fire and save the animals that were trapped in there. It even said to the big bird: "I don't need a consultant now. (Master laughs.) All I need is help! I need water! I don't need those empty statements from a consultant."

It kept on going about it's business, not caring about the big, pretty bird. This big bird, who was actually a god from heaven, was very touched to see how the parrot sacrificed itself for the animals of the world. The big bird was not able to forgive itself. The god felt ashamed and thought: "What am I doing with all this blessing and enjoyment that I have? Every day I just eat cookies, drink milk, enjoy nectar wine, being of no use whatsoever!"

He saw that this little animal had such a contributing, sacrificing spirit, so he was very ashamed of himself. He looked up to heaven. He saw the angels and gods enjoying themselves, looking down into the world full of pain and sorrow, thinking it was fun, like watching a show! He thought that he shouldn't live that way. Seeing this little parrot with so much compassion, with such a brave and sacrificing spirit, he thought that he should do something to help the parrot. It seemed like a better thing to do than to drink wine or milk and eat cookies every day in heaven and not do anything else.

Those are just heavenly blessings. A lot of people practice spiritually so they can go to heaven and live a very comfortable life. But this god thought that being in heaven enjoying the blessings was too boring and it made him feel ashamed. So he decided to help the parrot! He said: "I shall help the parrot!"

He thought of how touched he was, seeing how the parrot helped others to try to relieve their pain. He saw how the animals, running back and forth, were suffering. He was very moved, so he started to cry! He cried and cried; his tears were like rain. (Master laughs.) He was flying around and around crying, and his tears dropped like a heavy rain.

The forest fire quickly went out! The little parrot was also washed by the rain, and became pretty once again. It saw that it didn't have to work anymore, and that the animals were all out of danger. It started to laugh out loud. It sang: "Go! Go! Go!" (Master and everyone laugh. Applause)

The animals that were out of danger all knew that it was the little parrot that made this happen. They all saw the bird flying back and forth. They knew that was why the god was touched enough to come down and help. They were all singing, dancing, clapping, and cheering the parrot. And they all lived happily ever after, just like before! (Master laughs. Applause)


Although this story has a child's spirit, there are some things we can learn from it. Living in this world, no matter if it's for our home or for our country, we have to do whatever we can to help others. It's our duty. We don't have to talk about great things like pacifying the world. All we have to do is our daily activities well, then that's good.

So take care of your house, keep it tidy and nice looking to welcome your family members home; give the kids a clean environment and keep them healthy; then you have done your great duty. Sometimes when we see disasters somewhere, like floods, earthquakes, fires, we should do our best to help, just like what we often do. It's our duty. There are a lot of things we don't know about and can't help. But we do what we can do. We don't have to think: "There's so much suffering in the world. It would take forever for me to help." All you have to do is help with what's happening in front of you or with what you know about.

# Inner Feelings
## Of A
### Master

# The Story Of A *Bird*

This morning, before we left the house, there was a bird. It probably flew so fast it hit the glass window and dropped dead in front of my nose. That was the bad part, but the worst part was not that. There was another bird next to it — sat there, not moving for half an hour or a very long time, until I discovered both of them. It sat there because it was waiting for the other to get up and fly away with it. The way it sat there, didn't move one inch!

Normally birds, even if they sit, they would move their heads here and there. But that bird, it sat like it was dead, watching over the body of the other bird. Probably, it was too shocked to move or it was thinking, "Why don't you get up and fly away with me?" Maybe it knew that bird was already dead but it still waited, wondering whether it might get up. Looked like it was dead too because I walked up and down beside it, kept calling someone, and it never moved.

So I said to that person, "Come, maybe both of them are dead."

Then she just went near it, and it flew away — the other one. The one dead was still dead. I was so touched by the

58

faithfulness of the bird. The dead one was happy; but the live one, maybe it felt hurt now. The way it sat there and waited for the other to get up and fly away with it. They flew in together and suddenly one dropped dead; the other one just sat there and waited. Oh, it was too much for me.

So do not worry about your small question; it's not small for me, nothing is small. As far as a concerned person's point of view, it's not small. I don't know if that bird can find another companion or not. Probably it will fly up and down there, seeing if the other has gone. The female residents buried it.

# The Story Of A *Fly*

Restaurant

There was another story in India. Two months ago I went to India, just for a rest. I went back to the Himalayas. But it disappointed me so much this time. Everywhere was so dirty, not hygienic. People make toilets all along the banks of the river and you couldn't find a clean part of the river to sit and meditate. That was terrible. Everywhere was like that, and noisy. Thousands of pilgrims go there, and all kinds of cheap music. That was just by the way. Anyhow, I stayed there and meditated for some time. Since I was there, that's all, I stayed.

One day I went to a restaurant to eat something. Of course being alone, I didn't cook for myself. And over there, no problem, everywhere is vegetarian food. So at the restaurant, I saw a fly outside of the glass window, trapped in a cobweb. The way it was struggling, it hurt me. Of course I tried hard to rescue it. The window was fixed with nails so I could not open it – Indian style. I tried to open it with my fork and knife and things like that; I didn't succeed. I struggled for half an hour or so. One person sitting next to me, we just knew each other by the way. He was an Italian man. He said, "Don't bother about the fly. What is it? A fly, it's nothing."

I said, "Well, it's nothing for you, but it is something for me. Why do you interfere?"

He shook his head. He couldn't convince me of the unimportance of the life of a fly. Then we talked a little while, as I was trying in vain to save the fly. We were talking, he was trying to tell me to leave it, and I said to him, "The fly might not be important, but it is struggling in front of me and I see it. Now, if I can help, I should. Whether it is a fly or a person, what's the difference? It is the struggling, the suffering that you should eliminate. You don't care about the subject. I'd do it for the fly as well as for me, because I cannot bear to see the suffering."

We were talking and an Indian man came. He asked permission to sit next to me. I said, "Okay, it's a restaurant. Everyone can sit. (Master laughs.) Why ask me?"

He said, "Yes, because I want to talk to you."

"Ah!" I said, "What about?"

He tried to teach me the whole lesson about the unimportance of the life of a fly. He had his logic, no doubt. He said, "Excuse me, madam. But you must know that at this moment outside here, or everywhere in the world, thousands, millions of flies are dying. Why do you care for this small one?"

I said, "Yes, because it is dying in front of me and the other thousands I don't see. I cannot do anything about the thousands I don't know, but I can do what I know here. Otherwise, by the same logic, we see thousands and millions of people dying every day. Why should we care for anything at all? Why should we even care for our lives? Then we should stop eating and just die, by the same logic. Or we should not feed our children, because thousands of children are hungry in Africa. Why should we care for one or two children here, by the same logic?"

But he wasn't very happy. He tried to teach me more. I don't know. I was thinking maybe I must look like a very stupid person, so everyone always tries to teach me something. I was feeling terrible that the fly had to struggle for life. Then the man told me, "But by rescuing the fly, you take away the food from the spider."

"Yes, yes," I said, "but the spider is gone. The spider is not there."

He said, "How do you know?"

I said, "Because you can see that the web is mostly damaged and many dead bodies are already there. No one ate them. You can see that place is very windy and the spider could not live there very long. It has gone already. So many webs there and many dead bodies, but no one to benefit. Therefore, if I rescue the fly, it won't hurt the spider. Even if it were still there, there is still much more food there, too much for it already. No need one more victim for nothing. We should only eat when we feel hungry and take when we need."

Finally, they left me alone. They probably thought I was a very bad student, (Master laughs) not a potential disciple. So they left and that was that.

You see, I am not unsentimental. That makes my job harder, but I survive. Maybe half dead only, not completely dead. I have all the sentiments that you have; it's just that I know how to control them, if I want to and when necessary. Also, I know that these things are only fleeting moods of the mind. Sometimes I keep them to survive in this world, sometimes I suppress them, sometimes I ignore them. Depends on the situation. I cannot throw them away altogether. Otherwise, I cannot understand you, I cannot understand people. I have to keep all the human sentiments. I have to be both in heaven and on Earth. If I am too high, you cannot reach me and I cannot understand you.

In Buddhism, there is a sutra that's called Amitabha sutra. In that sutra, Shakyamuni Buddha described how beautiful the Pure Land is. In that Pure Land, apart from beautiful scenery, precious houses (which are made of crystal, diamonds, all kinds of precious stones), all kinds of beautiful precious flowers and all kinds of beautiful precious people who live there, there are other things. Everything is extraordinary.

But there is one thing very extraordinary about that land which is worth mentioning. That is, in that land, people have never heard of the word misery, never have had that kind of vocabulary, let alone know what misery or suffering is. If those people or that Buddha were to understand the suffering of this world, He, Himself, must suffer. If His consciousness were always fixed in the Pure Land, then He'd never hear of the word suffering, let alone know what suffering means.

So if someone tells you the Buddha is above suffering, is above sentiment, they are stupid eggs. They don't know what the Buddha is. What do we need a Buddha like that for? They might just as well worship a stone.

# The *Girl* Who Chose The **King**

**I**n India there is a story about a king. He was a very good king, loving to his subjects.

One day, he arranged that all his possessions, treasures were to be given to the people at large. Whoever needed anything could just come and satisfy him or herself at the exhibit without any condition at all. Because he had no children and no family ties, he loved his people as his own.

Everyone came and picked something of his hearts desire. But there was one girl, she came and went straight to the back of the place where the king was exhibiting all his possessions. She put her hand on his shoulder and asked, "Are you also available?"

The king was surprised and said, "Why? Don't you like any of the things that I have laid outside?"

The girl said, "No, I only like you." (Master laughs.)

Of course the king was very happy that someone like him for himself alone, and not because of his treasures. The king agreed, they got married, and they lived happily ever after, as it should be.

The girl did not want anything, but the whole nation now belonged to her, including all his subjects and all these objects.

# Love

## And

# Hatred

A long time ago there was a king whose name was Chang-Shou. It means long life in Chinese. However, he is not alive today. This is to let you know that this world is impermanent. (S.F. laughed.) One day King Chan-Shou wandered through his capital. He appeared very worried because his country was about to engage in war against a neighboring country.

This king was very fond of his fellow countrymen. He was a good king, a very shrewd king. He didn't like to see his countrymen being cruelly killed every day at war and didn't want to see the people bleeding and dying. So he was very hesitant and tried to avoid this situation. The king just walked to and fro in his palace, thinking of the unfortunate things which were about to happen the next day. This made him nervous, very sad and feel like crying very much.

Suddenly he recalled some words spoken to him by a very loyal, high ranking official. He said, "Your Majesty, don't hesitate too much. We have a well-trained and powerful army, and our country is prosperous and strong. I'm certain that we are able to fight well against them. Please do not hesitate anymore. We are all ready, and waiting for your order."

The more the king thought it over, the worse he felt; and he was unable to make a clear-cut decision. Since he had come to the throne, he had never used force with swords to rule his country. He ruled the country with love. So, his country was very peaceful and prosperous, and his people lived in peace and contentment. The people loved and respected the king very much, mainly due to the great love and high morality he had, but also because of his type of political system. Because of this, his country's army could not be very strong, very powerful. So he was not confident in winning the war.

It had never come to his mind that he should take over other countries or start a war with others. He had no idea of how to handle the situation he was confronting. Certainly, he might not win the battle if he sent out the troops. Also, if a war happened there would be deaths, causing his people's families to be ruined if their family members were killed. There would be a lot of damage both to his country and to his people. There would be widows and orphans after the war. He thought of the children, and what kind of sins they had committed? Why should they have to bear the suffering of the cruelty of war?

He kept thinking of these things, and felt so painful. He decided to go out to look for something more precious than any property or social status in the world. He intended to give away his country to the enemy. Perhaps he wanted to sit for meditation, to get initiation, to have a vegetarian diet. Then he walked around his palace to have a last look at his prince, the imperial concubines and beauties. They were still in deep sleep, not knowing that the country would change hands the next day.

The king went into the room of the prince to have a look at him. His name was "Chang-Shen (meaning everlasting in Chinese.) The "everlasting" lasts no longer and the "long life" has no life anymore. The king kept staring at his son. The prince was bent over his desk asleep after long hours of reading. This only son had been the king's only comfort, only spiritual support in the world to encourage him to live further since the queen had died. The prince wakened suddenly. When he saw his father, he greeted him.

The king talked to his son, "My son, the army of the neighboring country has reached our land and is intending to take our throne and country. However, I don't want to let my people plunge into an abyss of misery, just because I wish to keep the throne. The war will cause suffering to the people of the other country, and cause heavy damage, cause deaths to our country.

It's bad for the people of both countries. Therefore, I have decided to leave the throne to our neighbor. We had better go to the mountains to pursue spiritual practice."

When the prince learned that, he shed a few tears. I suppose he still yearned for the palace chocolates, blessed food, et cetera. How could he find blessed food if he went into the mountains? He certainly would not have the jelly candies anymore. Maybe he'd missed his home, where he lived since he was born, and then grew up. He never had to bear hardship before. But, at that moment, as he listened to his father, he realized that the glorious days were almost gone; and from then on, he would have to bear hardship and hard work.

The king and prince left and went to the mountains hand in hand. Then the king sat for meditation under a bodhi tree, practicing the Quan Yin Method. Maybe it was like that. After a time, they never heard another human voice; and gradually, they got used to this kind of life, feeling better and better without any yearning for the past glorious life.

The prince walked deep into the mountains every day to look for wild fruit and edible plants. Then, he brought them back to offer to his father. One day the prince went out again, leaving his father sitting for meditation alone. Suddenly the king heard an excited voice coming from the side, "It's him, it's him, he is the king."

Then he saw a thin and small ugly man jump out of the bushes. The man told the king, "Our palace has been taken by the enemy. Many officials have committed suicide to show their loyalty. The rest have quit their positions and gone back to their home towns to do farming. The king of the neighboring country has given orders to seize all of you. Our people are suffering greatly, not knowing when it will end. I have traveled many places in the country to find you, almost everywhere. I am so glad that I could find you today.

At this time the king was feeling so miserable, he burst into tears, asking, "Our people have plunged into great sorrow because I went away?"

The man said, "Yes, because you escaped, the king of the enemy country gave orders to capture, question, and torture them severely in order to know where you went. But, no one knew. The king of the enemy country had suspected that our people were hiding you some place; therefore, he cruelly beat many people. The new king has promised to give a handsome reward to anyone who can give a tip as to your whereabouts."

Then the man grabbed King Chang-Shou's arm, saying, "You come back with me right now. I want to get my reward."

The king pushed him away, and the skinny man fell to the ground. The king was about to reprimand him but then he thought, "How can I be so hardhearted so as to let my people suffer so much for me. My body is impermanent."

Even though his name was "Chang-Shou," he realized that life is impermanent. The king thought, "I can keep this body today, but perhaps it will be ruined tomorrow. If I go back and let my opponent capture me, then I can save many innocent people."

The king patted the man's shoulder slightly and said, "Okay, you can take me back, because you will be satisfied and many people will be happy."

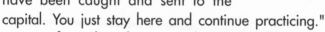

He didn't resist going back. Then, King Chang-Shou used a stone to carve some words onto the trunk of a tree, to say good-bye to the prince. The king was afraid that the prince's mind would be in turmoil when he returned and found that the king wasn't there. The king wrote, "I have been caught and sent to the capital. You just stay here and continue practicing."

After asking his son to keep on with his spiritual practice instead of running after him, the king left with the man. The little man just kept hurrying the king to move faster. The man was really an ignorant being. Even in that situation, he didn't feel affected at all. His vicious mind couldn't understand the way a spiritual practitioner would think. His greed for worldly fortune made him blind, covered his eyes, and also made his mind dull.

The prince came out from the mountains with a basket of fruit and vegetables for his father, but he couldn't find him. He called but he didn't get any response. Suddenly, he saw the words carved on the tree by his father. He burst into tears.

70

His father no longer had desire for worldly wealth.

The king had drifted here and become a spiritual practitio-ner. He practiced under a tree and was never interested in mun-dane affairs, never longed for worldly wealth. He never wanted to get his throne back. In order to reduce the cruel killing of his people by the enemy, and to lessen the suffering of the people, the king had left his palace without hesitation! Still, there were people coming to grab him, and wanting to kill him. The prince was feeling that the people of the secular world were so vicious, so cruel, far beyond his imagination.

The king and prince had lived in such a desolate area without anyone else around; they just lived by eating wild fruit and drinking water from the stream. They lived such a peaceful life, yet people still came to capture them and wanted to kill them. The prince began crying because he couldn't understand the cruelity of the world at all.

When King Chang-Shou was taken back to the capital, the king of the enemy country wasted no time starting a fire to put him to death. Many people of his country gathered around the execution area. They were so sad that they broke into tears, because they knew that he was a good king and that he loved his people. The people were crying not only because of the king's death, but also because he was a kindhearted, decent, moral and loving person. The prince hid himself among those sad, crying people. He couldn't help coming to take a last look at his father, even though his father wished him to stay in the mountains to continue with his spiritual practice.

The prince didn't dare to cry out loudly. He sent a signal to his father with his hands to let the king know that he was there. At the same time, the soldiers started the fire. King Chan-Shou was about to die at any moment. When the king saw the prince there with hatred flaming in his eyes, he became very worried, feeling that something would go wrong because the prince was saying in his heart to the king that he would absolutely revenge his father's death. King Chang-Shou tried to advise the prince.

About to die, he still tried to tell the prince. But he didn't dare to speak in the direction of the place where the prince was standing, so he spoke into the air, "Chang-Shen, you have to use love to wash away the hatred. You shouldn't return a sword with a sword. You should live a life like a Buddha or a Bodhisattva, with mercy and love, without thinking of hatred or violence."

Then the king died, engulfed by the strong flames. The prince lost consciousness. He was too angry and heart-broken. He was only fourteen years old then. He was so young when he witnessed his father's torturous death. You can imagine how he felt when he saw his father being ruthlessly killed. Of course he couldn't bear it. The more he remembered his father's death, the more he wanted to revenge. He thought, "That guy took over our territory and killed my father. I definitely have to take revenge on him. I have to!"

His mind was completely occupied by the idea of killing, leaving no room for thinking or anything else. He was hungry and cold, but he had no place to go. The more he felt hungry, cold and the hardship, the more he got angry and wanted re-venge. Then he had a plan to come as close to the enemy king as possible.

He drifted along in the capital city, trying to get a job. A minister of the enemy country happened to see him. Thinking he was young and having good strength, he hired the prince to help him plant vegetables, water flowers, and take care of the garden. The prince was very smart and diligent. Very soon, the minister's whole family were fond of him. The minister and his subordinates all trusted and liked the prince very much, treating him as the most favoured one, entrusting him with many things. The minister had no idea that the young man was Prince Chang-Shen, because the prince was proficient in make-up and he altered his looks.

One day, the minister asked the prince, "Do you have other talents besides the ones I have already seen."

The prince said, "I am a very good cook."

He really was a good cook. He cooked even better than any of the other chefs in the minister's residence. Therefore, the minister favored the prince even more. Because the minister was very proud of Prince Chang-Shen, he invited the king to come over to eat. He intended to praise his new cook for his cooking skill and intelligence. When the day came, the prince tried his best to prepare the most delicious delicacies for the king. I don't know if what he cooked were meat dishes or vegetable dishes. The new king appreciated Prince Chang-Shen very much, both as a young man and for his cooking. Then the king asked the minister, "Please give him to me."

The king asked the minister to let Prince Chnag-Shen cook for him, and come near to him. Of course, the minister would not dare refuse this request; he had no choice but to give his most favorite and trusted subordinate to the king. Then Prince Chang-Shen became the king's chef. In order to gain the king's trust in him as much as possible, Prince Chang-Shen tried his best to cheer up the king every day, to make him happy, and to cook good food for him. He did everything very respectfully, cautiously to serve the king well. The king became more and more fond of him.

Because Prince Chang-Shen was very clever and sharp, and had a lot of talents, the king liked him very much. Then Prince Chang-Shen became the king's bodyguard and the king's most

trusted person. He asked Chang-Shen's
advice for almost everything. Since the
prince was born and raised in the palace,
he was very familiar with many things
with respect to the palace. He knew
how to organize things, and what
should happen there. He could
handle everything.

One day, the prince
thought the day he had
been longing for had
come. The king took
Prince Chang-Shen
on a hunting trip. The
king chased after an animal and went deep into the mountains.
All of the rest were left far behind, as the king was riding the best
horse. The king and Prince Chang-Shen pursued the prey deep
into the mountains. Prince Chang-Shen knew the way out, but he
intentionally misled the king so that he'd get lost in the mountains.
Then he pretended to have no idea how to get out.

As night fell, they still couldn't find their way out. Perhaps
the king was too tired. He couldn't help lying down to take a rest.
There were tall trees all around, and the trails were narrows and
led in different directions. Prince Chang-Shen stood beside the
king holding a sword to "protect" him. Now Chang-Shen's rare
opportunity had come. Chang-Shen reminded himself, and glanced
at the enemy deep in sleep. The king slept so sweetly and so
deeply beside Chang-Shen. His brain kept on pushing him, "He
killed your father, overtook your throne. You have to hurry to send
him to death."

74

The king didn't practice the Quan Yin Method, but he could also be liberated! Just cutting him into two pieces with a sword would be okay. Prince Chang-Shen hesitated. He thought of his father's advice, but his brain reminded him again, "What are you waiting for? Hurry up and kill him."

This is the way the brain is. The brain always urges us to do bad things, doesn't it? Even a practitioner like Chang-Shen was no exception. Because he was young and had witnessed what had happened to his father, he felt it was unfair.

Prince Chang-Shen pulled out his sword to get ready. He wasn't going to cut the weeds! Instead, he planned to stab the king's wisdom eye. Suddenly the scene of his father being ruthlessly burned returned to his mind. At that time, his father said to him with eyes full of mercy and love, "My son, you have to wash hatred with love. You should follow the way of the Buddhas and learn how to be merciful and loving. You shouldn't behave ruthlessly."

When he thought of this, his heart melted with compassion. He said, "How can I ignore my father's last request. If I do, I wouldn't be filial."

His father was so compassionate and merciful. He should follow his father's example, instead of doing the opposite. When the prince thought about this, he slowly put his sword back into its scabbard. He just stood there and cried. Then the new king opened his eyes, saying to Prince Chang-Shen, "I just had a bad dream. I saw someone trying to kill me."

Prince Chang-Shen answered, "Perhaps it was because you fell asleep on the cool ground and that made you have a bad dream. I am protecting you, no one would dare kill you."

The new king felt very secure and lay down to rest again. Prince Chang-Shen stood guard. When he thought of his father

75

being brutally killed, the hatred emerged again. His brain pushed him, "Kill him, kill him, kill him. He killed your father, you have to take revenge."

His brain pushed him again and again. He pulled out his sword, held it up high, and wielded it down almost to the king's head. His father's words returned to him once more, "You shouldn't be so ruthless. You have to wash away the hatred with love... et cetera."

He couldn't sustain the struggle with his feelings and shouted out very loudly, showing that he was very angry. The prince then said to the king, "You, the most ruthless enemy, I forgive you. For the sake of my father, for his merciful love, I forgive you!"

Then, he put his sword back in its original place, where it "rests," and it never came out again. Mercy had overcome hatred. Suddenly, the king awoke again! He always awakened in time, almost losing his life. He said, "My dear, I had another bad dream. I dreamt about the son of the former king forgiving my sin. He ceased his revenge. Do you know what this dream means?"

Prince Chang-Shen said to the king with his eyes full of tears, "I am the son of the former king. When my father was burned to death by you, he asked me not to return hatred with hatred, and to use love to wash away hatred. He wanted me to follow the way of the Buddhas' merciful love, and treat all beings with this kind love. I intended to kill you, but I couldn't do it."

The king was filled with regret. He held Prince Chang-Shen and cried. The two men cried together. The king said, "Alright, please kill me to revenge your father. You don't have to struggle with it anymore and give yourself even more pain."

The king's stone-like nature melted away. He was enlightened to some extent. He was willing to be killed by Prince Chang-

Shen. He didn't want him to struggle any longer, revealing that he also had feelings of love. That touched Prince Chang-Shen very much. He said, "No, your Majesty, I won't kill you. As a subordinate, I dare not do it. Please punish me."

The two men decided not to kill each other and they became very quiet. Suddenly they were enlightened. Just as when the sun comes up, they felt the darkness inside had gone. The merciful light seemed to shine through the whole world. The king held his head, thinking the sins which he had committed were too heavy and Prince Chang-Shen was so noble, so merciful. He felt very ashamed. All of a sudden, the king realized something, and felt very delighted with it. He was enlightened and told Prince Chang-Shen, "My dear, today I really found out what the most beautiful thing in the world is. War and hatred are sinful and vicious. Only love is the true treasure."

Prince Chang-Shen led the king out of the forest. The many high ranking officials there were worried. They had no idea where the king had gone. When the king and Prince Chang-Shen came back to the capital, the king asked his officials, "Do you know where the prince of the former king is?" Of course no one knew. The king lifted Prince Chang-Shen's hand very high, saying, "It's him! He is the prince of the former king. He is my preceptor too. He didn't kill me. Instead, he taught me a great lesson. Through him I have come to realize the noble moral qualities of the former king. I want to follow his example."

The king returned to his former country, and ruled his country with love. He also returned the occupied territory to Prince Chang-Shen, and Prince Chang-Shen used his father's compassion and love as a guide to rule his country. His country became more and more prosperous and peaceful. So the suffering of our world was reduced in one more corner, and there was one more bright and peaceful place. That is the end of the story.

Shakyamuni Buddha in a previous life was King Chang-Shou. That was the way He spoke. Prince Chang-Shen was Ananda, and the king of the enemy country was Devadatta in that previous life. No wonder he always tried to hurt Shakyamuni Buddha. He tried to kill Him in every life. Wherever Shakyamuni Buddha went, Davadatta always tried to kill him.

# Disaster Begins
## With The
### *Mouth*

Long time ago, there was a lake in some place. Near that lake, there was a turtle and two flamingos. They were friends. That year there was a kind of drought, so no water. For one year, no rain whatsoever; and the water in the lake became less and less each day. They had no water now. The sun seemed to become hotter and hotter than usual. All the grass and the trees had changed color, become coffee color, some kind of black. Then, because the water had become so little, and the sun was so hot, the water kind of became very, very hot. So, those living inside the aquarium, slowly went to nirvana, one by one.

Now, in this kind of situation, the turtle was very restless; and he was always thinking many things in his head about what to do. He wanted very much to be liberated from this situation. He thought and thought! Then, fortunately, the flamingo couple came to visit him. Seeing him with such a miserable Buddha face, wearing such a miserable Buddha mask, they asked him in a very friendly, anxious, considerate, loving way, "What's going on? What's the matter with you? Why do you look so miserable?"

The turtle said to them, "Oh! Oh! Y-You-have-no-idea! I'm in a great pre-di-ca-ment! Ah! I think I am going to die. I don't think I'll ever see you again. Hur..."

Then, the husband flamingo interrupted him and said, "We have been good friends for a long time. We've shared our happiness and troubles for a very long time. Please let us know what is making you so unhappy and worried. We will surely try our best to help you, to rescue you out of your miserable condition. We do not even know what the problem is, and you are already so disappointed, and so hopeless. You should not be this way. Every problem has a solution."

Sounds very wise indeed. Maybe he practices the Quan Yin Method. Enlightened flamingos. Ah! Okay! Let's see.

The turtle sighed miserably, out of the depths, and answered them, "I don't know-what-you-can-do-for-me, you two. But... for many days... I haven't had anything to put into my solar plexus center. All I can do is meditate on the solar plexus center. There has been no enlightenment. So, I think I'm going to die. Ah! No water, no fish, no frogs, nothing. I think I'm going to die. Or eventually the cowboys will discover me, and bring me for their soup... Once, five years ago, I was caught by them. Luckily there was an old lady who believed in Buddhism. So, she bought me and returned me to the lake. If I'm caught again, I'm not sure if Amitabha can rescue me. Maybe Suma Ching Hai can do it. I have not tried Her, I don't know. Ah! Anytime I think of my last escape, I grow goose pimples all over my shell."

Now the husband flamingo was very, very deep in meditation over the problem. So, his eyebrows were knitted together like this, his legs were crossed like that, his wings were placed on top of his legs in a flamingo position, and his wisdom eye was kind of clouded in color from thinking. Also his wife, the female flamingo, was so much in sympathy with the turtle. Then he said, "Why don't you move to another place, move your house?"

The turtle, in his very deep misery, just said to the flamingo, "Imagine, I have never been anywhere else. I don't even have a car. You know my movements are not very fast. Without a car, what shall I do? Besides, I love my hometown. I would rather die in my motherland. If I'm buried in some strange place, do you think my soul will not become restless?"

Suddenly, the husband flamingo raised his very long neck. "I have an idea, I want to speak, please," he said. Full of hope and inspiration he continued to say, "Ah! Don't fear, don't fear. I know ten miles away from here there is a lotus pond, and that pond is famous for never being dried up. Even when we have had such a drought as this, it has never dried up. We will bring you over there. Then we will be with you, so that you don't feel lonely. We'll share every up and down with you. Is that alright?"

The turtle considered. He is very slow even in thinking. He thought in his turtle manner, yet wise. He kept thinking for maybe half an hour, until he thought it over. Turtles are very slow. He said, "Now, even ten meters I couldn't go, never mind ten miles. I have had nothing to eat. Ten meters I couldn't move. Ten miles!?"

Looked like he was going to die. Then, the flamingo said, "Don't worry! We already knew. We have transportation for you. We have booked you a first-class air ticket. Don't worry, don't worry. But, there is a condition. You have to listen carefully to our plan. Then, we can do it."

The turtle was very seriously interested. He said, "Yes, yes, please." Now he was quick. He answered in twenty minutes instead of half an hour. "Please tell me, please."

The flamingo said, "Here, it's very simple. We both pick up a string. We bite the both ends of the string, and you bite in the middle. Then, we will carry you to the destination. But, you must know never to open your mouth during the journey. Otherwise, it would be dangerous. Maybe your shell will not be in order – one piece in one place, or maybe become turtle powder smashed into mashed potatoes. It doesn't matter what happens in between, no matter how excited, how angry or how you are provoked, you must never, ever open your mouth. And in only half an hour, we'll be there. So you remember."

The flamingo made sure once more, "Remember, clinch your teeth, don't talk. Don't even yawn. You can't even ha-chu (sneeze). You have to be patient, control yourself, until we reach the destination. Everything is fixed, ready, understood, stand by, and good luck!"

Then, both of them bit the two ends of the string, and the turtle in the middle. They moved from one place to another. They flew over green pastures, red flowers, coffee dried grass, like in California when we last visited and then it became green after one week or two. So many beautiful scenes passed by. The turtle enjoyed so much that he forgot his home sickness. Many times he wanted to open his mouth just to praise the surroundings! Oh! Beautiful Christmas trees! Lovely chapatis! Tasty Indian tea! Beautiful Au Lac ladies! Nice Chinese songs! Lovely water! But he remembered. He remembered what the flamingo had said to him – that he couldn't open his mouth for any reason whatsoever. So, he controlled hard, pulled all his attention in his mouth, and never opened it.

But... there is always a "but". But, they flew over one village where there were children. And you know children, they are always very naughty. When they saw the two flamingos and the turtle together, they began shouting, jumping, and making fun of the turtle. Now, the turtle could not bear anymore. Never, ever in his life, having lived to such an old age, had people or anyone disrespected him like this. His ego got hurt! His self-esteem ran low battery, his wisdom twisted, and his pride boiled up like when you're cooking at two hundred degrees in the oven. So, he flashed his turtle eyes down to the Earth, and he opened his turtle mouth, and said to them, "Shut up! Shut your very mouth!"

As he said that, he became no more turtle! He was liberated! He was freed from his shell!

So, the Buddha said, "In this world how many people just because they don't keep their mouths shut, they run into disasters like that. Therefore, take heed that you talk only when necessary." The story speaks for itself.

# Trust The Master

# POWER

This is an Indian story. There was a woman who practiced very well spiritually. Many people were jealous of her because she was very much liked and respected. Even the king was jealous of her. Many people heard about her practice and did not believe that a woman could practice so well. Therefore, the king asked someone to take her to the palace, with the intent to insult her.

Under such circumstances, being pressured and pushed too hard, she tried to escape this difficult situation. She kept trying with her own mind, but in vain. Occasionally, she remembered to call her master, once or a couple of times; mostly out of habit, not very sincerely. She was still trying to use her own power, not believing completely that the master could save her. While asking for her master's help, she was still trying to struggle, not truly, sincerely asking for her master's help, not leaving everything for her master to take care of. That's why her master didn't show up.

Finally, there was nothing else she could do. She surrendered and wholeheartedly relied on her master. She said, "No matter what happens now, master, please take care of it."

At that moment, her master came in the form of a light body and saved her immediately.

Most of the time, it's more difficult if we struggle with our own strength. Who is the master? Actually, it's also our own power, the higher-Self, the perfect self-being who knows everything, who is omnipresent, and omnipotent. If we use our own mind, we are just relying on that low conscious self, just our past experiences.

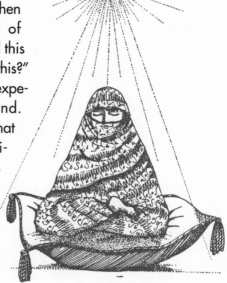

For example, "What should I do when I encounter a certain situation? How should I react when I encounter certain types of people? I have encountered this before, how should I handle this?" All of this is using the past experiences stored in our mind. However, you should know that sometimes the past experiences are different from this one, because the situation is different. Sometimes, just a subtle difference will make it totally different.

The
Enlightened
FAIRIES

There is a story in India. It seems that the Chinese have a similar story. One day, the King of Hell organized a very big party. He invited the ghosts, gods and fairies to come to eat together. The King of Hell was very naughty (this was his character). He purposely put many delicacies in the middle, with the chairs very far from the table and very long ladles in the dishes. All the choice delicious food from the mountains and the sea – heavenly peaches, grape wine and everything you could think of, was there. It was the most delectable and the best, making everyone's mouth water.

However, the King of Hell had one condition: While eating, one could not bend one's elbow. Normally, one should bend one's elbow when eating. The ladle was that long, the table was so far away, the elbow could not be bent, and yet they were told that they could eat everything. Those ghosts, astral beings complained, quarreled, scolded the King of Hell, and then they all left! Only the fairies stayed behind to think about a method. In a second, they understood! They began to spoonfeed one another. Thus, there was no violation of the rule, no need to bend the elbow, and yet they were able to eat. There was a difference between the enlightened fairies and the ghosts.

For us ordinary people, if we could not eat, then we'd create havoc so that others also could not eat. As a result, both could not eat. This is the quality of Maya. Although we have the human body, some of us are Maya. If our actions are like Maya's, then we are Maya. Without a spirit of sacrifice – what we cannot have, others also cannot have – there is only destruction. Just like the ghosts, pressuring each other but not taking care of one another.

When we take care of others, God will also take care of us. I can guarantee this. During practice, don't be afraid of losing business. One should learn the spirit of those fairies. The ladles were that long, and to spoonfeed each other must have been very easy and lots of fun. They must have played happily. Everyone was laughing. But those ghosts went back with empty stomachs, very angry, and were not able to eat anything.

An enlightened person lives very comfortably, because we are able to see through things and think clearly. If we are not enlightened, maintaining our mood all the time, thinking, "I am the most important person," then there will be a lot of trouble! Thinking that there are no other people in the world, only "me" alone, we must bear the sufferings ourselves; happiness can also be enjoyed by "me" alone. In this way, this would be a nonsense realm.

# A Mother's Advice

EAT WELL BROTH

**A** daughter who was betrothed to her husband went far away. Then before she left for her husband's house her mother gave her very, very good advice. The mother didn't cry and did not let the daughter cry. Instead she said, "You must listen to me. This is a very happy day. God has blessed you with a good husband who even practices the Quan Yin Method, (Master and everyone laugh), who doesn't gamble, who doesn't fool around with other women, who doesn't drink, who doesn't cheat; but who's honest, charitable, gentle, moral, virtuous and handsome (everyone laughs) inside and outside."

Inside he was more beautiful than outside. Inside he was white, even though outside he was black. (Master and everyone laugh.)

The daughter smiled and listened with care, love and attention to the mother. The mother said, "Now, you go to your new home. Treat your relatives-in-law as your own. Respect your mother and father-in-law as you have respected me and your father. Respect your husband as your only God, guru, friend, protector, and the most beloved and respected person on the Earth planet so that later you'll make a shining example for your children and bring glory, happiness

and pride to your new family. You owe that to your husband, to myself, your father and all your sisters and brothers in our family to fulfill this duty. You owe it to yourself as well as your husband to glorify all of us in this way.

"Take care of your family, your husband's property and business so that it'll prosper, and it'll bring loftiness, security and abundance to your family so that your children will live in comfort. There's nothing to be sad about today, there's only the exciting future and new challenge awaiting you. To be loved by a husband is the most beautiful thing in the world. You should endeavour to be a good wife, so that you have all this happiness and success in your life."

The daughter said, "But what can I do to fulfill all these noble obligations and this beautiful duty that you have just told me about?"

The mother said, "You must eat well, dress beautifully, and sleep soundly every day."

The daughter said, "Yes mother, I understand."

So when she went to the family-in-law, she did exactly that – slept well, ate well, dressed beautifully every day. All the family members-in-law were so happy with her. She raised beautiful, obedient, clever, hard working, hard studying children for the husband and the family-in-law.

Other people came and asked for her secret, "How did you do it? You came from such a far away place, you knew nothing about the customs of this land, and yet, you did so well. How did you do it?"

The daughter-in-law, now proud mother of three, matriarch of the family, female boss of the husband's company, secretary-in-chief, housekeeper of the whole household, (Master and everyone laugh) a nurse to the elders and fragile mother and father-in-law, a family leader for the younger brothers and sisters-in-law et cetera, and an assistant but loving mother of three beautiful, healthy, intelligent children, said very humbly, "I achieved all this due to the loving advice of my mother."

Everyone of course said, "Give me, give me please – tell me, tell me, tell me."

"My mother told me before I came here a sad bride, that I should go to my family-in-law and sleep soundly, eat very well, and dress chic." (Master and everyone laugh.)

Everyone said, "What? What kind of advice was that? And you did exactly just that to run your family?"

She said, "Yes, I did exactly just that – ate well, slept soundly, and dressed chic every day. That's what I did."

They said, "How? What do you mean? By just enjoying this, you ran your family and everything went along well? Please explain to us. Are you joking or something?"

She said, "No! No! What my mother meant by eating well was that I must take care of the whole family, feed them all, including the guests, until they are all full and satisfied. Then I eat myself what is left over; because after everyone is satisfied, no one will disturb me anymore. (Master laughs.) I'll be hungry by then (everyone laughs) – having run around – so whatever is left over, doesn't matter what, will be very tasty, delicious, (everyone laughs) nourishing and will have a lot of blessing power.

"I pray to Suma Ching Hai before I eat (Master and everyone laugh) and She blesses my food. So whatever I eat becomes nectar. My body is strong, my palate is satisfied, my heart is contented so I can offer my best service to my family after I'm well fed, satisfied, and have enjoyed a delicious meal in all quietness and tranquility. When everyone is satisfied and full, they also love me; and of course, their loving feelings also bless me as well

93

because I took care of them very well. All their good wishes and their contented feelings bless me and I share the merit of their happiness as well. So that's the secret of eating well."

Then they said, "You sleep every night soundly? You just worry about sleep?"

She said, "No! What my mother meant by sleeping well is that, after everyone is asleep, I take care of all the doors, turn off all the lights, make sure everything is in place and secured so that the thieves do not come in; take care of all the family members that everyone is well, sound asleep. Then I don't worry. Then my heart is very calm and relaxed because I know they are all well taken care of and warm in their blankets; that they'll sleep all night long and they will never get up and disturb me, ask for anything, or be sick. Then I don't have to worry. I sleep myself very soundly too because there's nothing else to do. (Master and everyone laugh.) That's what my mother meant."

The others were feeling very surprised and impressed about the wisdom of the mother, as well as the wisdom of the daughter. Of course, like mother like daughter.

94

"Now about the last one, please, about the last one. Oh! Why do you have to dress well?"

So she said, "Yes! Dressing well means you have to be always properly dressed and tidy. You dress yourself with a big smile when you wake up in the morning and the last thing before you go to bed. You dress yourself with all the loving kindness that God has bestowed within your heart; so when people see you, they see an angel, they see love written in your face, they see blessings shinning in your eyes, they see God in your benevolent smile. That's what my mother meant by dressing well.

"That's how I dress myself every day. That's how I feed myself to health every day. That's how I sleep with sweet dreams every night. If all of you do that, your family members, your in-laws, will also be as well as mine right here!"

Everyone of course bowed, clapped, smiled, dressed them-selves well, and went home.

95

# PRINCE VICTORIOUS

## And The

# Five Hundred Beggars

Now, there is a story concerning one of the Buddha's previous lives. In that lifetime, He was a householder named Pacifier.

At one time, thus I have heard, the Enlightened One was residing in the city of Sarasvati at the Chettavana Ashram in "Annatakapikitikakapaka". You know already that place? Very difficult to pronounce. (Laughter) At that time, there were five hundred beggars in that vicinity who relied upon the Buddha and the sangha for sustenance.

I wonder how they did that? Probably they came and ate the leftovers; or maybe they came and hung around to see everyone who offered food to the sanghas and the Buddha, then they probably partook of some of it. That could have been done too.

One day, in Chettavana Park, suddenly the five hundred beggars came to the Buddha and begged Him to ordain them into monkhood. They said to Him, "Compassionate Lord, through Your mercy and the mercy of the brotherhood, we have been fed. Now we desire that You bestow great merit upon us and let us become sangha members."

That means to become monks.

The Buddha said to them, "The dharma which I teach is totally pure and makes no distinction between race or caste, between rich or poor, between good or bad. It is like washing in pure water. Water washes all races and castes, rich and poor, good and bad without distinction. It is like the fire which burns all substances without exception – mountain, rock, sky and earth. My teachings are like the sky under which all find a place – men, women, boys, girls, rich, poor, all without exception."

Of course, that meant he accepted the beggars to become monastic disciples.

97

Now the beggars rejoiced and believed when they heard what the Lord had said. Then they again requested permission to join the order. Perhaps that was the etiquette of the old times. You had to request the Buddha twice or three times to show your sincerity and earnestness in following Him. So at this time, the Lord said, "Welcome."

Their hair and busks fell away. They were dressed in the yellow robes of the order and became monks. When the Lord had instructed them in the dharma, their minds became liberated, their outflows were stopped, and they became arhats.

When certain high-caste householders, merchants and princes, who lived in that country, heard that the wretched beggars had been accepted into the order, they were very offended. They said to each other, "If we were to invite the Buddha and the noble sangha in order to create virtue, these beggars would also sit above us and we would have to give obeisance to them, et cetera. Then we would be dishonoured."

It means they defied them, the beggars' sangha.

So upon a certain occasion, Prince Victorious invited the Buddha and the sangha. But he said to the Buddha first, "Oh Lord! I have invited the Buddha and the sangha, but those beggars who have lately become monks are not invited."

He made a distinction. Do you think it was good? No, it was not good.

The next day, when it was time for the Lord and His disciples to go to the prince's house, the Buddha told those monks who had not been invited, "The master of gifts has not invited you. Do go to the northern continent and obtain wild rice that has been neither sown nor reaped. Bring it to the master of gifts' house and eat it there."

Immediately, in accordance with the Buddha's command, they flew with the spiritual powers of the arhats to the northern continent and filled their begging bowls with rice. Then in beautiful formation like wild geese in the sky, they flew back to the palace of Prince Victorious, sat down in a row, and ate the special rice. When Prince Victorious saw the monks come flying through the sky in lovely formation, he was astonished, rejoiced, and believed. Then he asked the Buddha, "Oh Lord! Where have these magnificent, splendid, virtuous, holy, wise men come from?"

The Buddha said, "You should recognize them. Listen well prince, I shall tell you about them. These monks are those whom you did not invite. Because you did not invite them, they had to go to the northern continent and obtain wild rice to eat."

Wow! Terrible. How do you think you'd feel if you were Prince Victorious in this case? Feel good? Ashamed? Terrible?

When Prince Victorious heard this, he was overcome with shame. Well, you are very intelligent! You guessed correctly. He was very ashamed of himself. He repented what he had done, and said to the Buddha, "It was because I was obstructed by ignorance that I did not understand about these holy men and refused to invite them. Lord, Your virtue is beyond conception. Although these holy men were low-caste beggars in this country,

through the Lord's mercy, they have found joy in the world and have obtained benefits for a long time to come. Oh Lord! Your coming into this world is for such as these. I beg You to explain what root of virtue these beggars planted in order to meet You and attain liberation, and because of what former sins were they first born as beggars."

This is concerning karma.

So the Buddha explained like this, "In times long passed, eons beyond recall, there was a mountain called Many Reshis. At one time, when there were two thousand reshis living on the mountain, a soothsayer foretold that for twelve years there would be no rain." (A reshi is someone who has attained a lot of magical powers, including flying through the air perhaps, seeing through thousands of miles, seeing through walls and obstacles, and things like that. They are very virtuous too. That's why they are called reshis.) "The reshis, thereupon, went to a wealthy householder by the name of Pacifier, who lived in that land. They asked if he would offer them food and drink for twelve years; and if he would not, they would go elsewhere.

"The householder told them, 'Holy reshis! Do not go any-where else. Remain here, I beg you; and I shall make offerings for twelve years.'"

Because there would not be rain for twelve years, the reshis came to this householder and asked him for a secure offering for twelve years.

"The householder then asked his treasurer if there were enough supplies to feed the holy men for twelve years. When told that there were enough, the householder appointed five hundred men to serve the reshis. When the five hundred men had served for some time, they became tired, and began to murmur among themselves that it was too much trouble to care for the beggars.

"Now at that time, there was a certain man who called the reshis at mealtime and he had a dog that followed him. One day, the man forgot to call the reshis. But the dog ran to them, began to bark, and the reshis knew that the food was ready and went to receive it. Some time later, the reshis told the householder that the rains were soon coming and that he must prepare his fields for the sowing of the seeds. The householder directed his field workers to begin work in the fields.

"They planted barley, wheat and many other kinds of crops. When the seeds had sprouted and grown as high as water pots, the householder went to the reshis and asked if there would be a good yield. The reshis said that the crops would be good and advised him to irrigate from time to time. When the crops were harvested, it was found that the yield was many fold; and the householder rejoiced when his storeroom was filled.

"When the five hundred men who had served the reshis saw this manifestation of their power, they felt very ashamed, felt very remorseful, and confessed to the holy men, saying 'Holy Ones! We humiliated you with our evil words and we confess our sin. In future times, may we again meet you and attain liberation.'

"It was because of those evil words against the reshis that those five hundred men were reborn as miserable beggars for five hundred lifetimes. Later, by having confessed their sin and having made a vow, they met me and reached the end of the circle of birth and death.

"Prince, you should understand this. I was the householder called Pacifier. Udiyana was the treasurer. (Udiyana was one of the Buddha's disciples at that time.) And you, Prince Victorious, were the man who daily called the reshis at mealtime. You whose name is Good Voice were the dog. (There was a person next to the prince called Good Voice.) Because you called the holy men once only, by barking at that mealtime, you have a good voice throughout all your lifetimes. These five hundred beggars were the five hundred serving men at that time."

When the Buddha had thus spoken, some in the great assembly attained from the first to the fourth fruits. Some brought forth a mind of supreme enlightenment. All had faith in the words of the Lord and rejoiced in their hearts.

Most of the stories in this book tell us how much benefit one would derive from offering anything to the sangha members or to people who are practicing spiritual meditation. Even the reshis, they were not perhaps the Buddha, but they followed the way of righteousness and the way of Truth. They practiced and attained wisdom to a certain extent, and they would not stray to the evil path. Therefore, these people are worthy of the offerings of sentient beings.

Whoever makes offerings to these people will attain a lot of virtues, merit throughout all their lives in the material existence, finally meet a living Buddha, and attain liberation or the supreme enlightenment. Even a dog, out of a good heart, barked at the reshis just to tell them that the meal was ready. Because it did only that thing, it was born as a human being many, many lifetimes, and had a beautiful voice. Finally, he met the Buddha, when He was born in India; and also practiced with Him together with the prince.

Now Prince Victorious, normally he would not have generated such a discriminating mind toward any sangha members, be they beggars or noble persons. But it was because of the bad karma of the beggars in the previous lifetime. Do you remember? It occurred when they were serving the reshis under the Buddha when He was a layman. Therefore, because they had earned this bad karma, when they met Prince Victorious, he intuitively felt that these people were not to be included in his invitation. Nevertheless, even though it was karma, Prince Victorious should not have discriminated. It wasn't even his fault, so we can't blame him. It was the karma of the five hundred beggars in the previous lifetime. Therefore, you see, whatever happens to us, it's not without cause.

This story teaches us patience, acceptance and endurance in whatever test in life the Lord of Karma has chosen to bestow upon us in order to cleanse us of our previous sins, our previous mistakes. First, the five precepts – that we keep, of course, including loving kindness, endurance, patience and all that. They are there so that we do not sow bad seeds for the future. And whatever bad karma in the past, we will just patiently, lovingly accept until it is finished. For example, in this story, the five hundred beggars, even though they had done very bad deeds in their past life, they repented. So the deeds of the past life left them for good, after the five hundred lifetimes of paying their retribution for their deeds.

Now even just to feel that they were lazy a few times, to feel that the reshis were not worthy of veneration and offering, just to feel in their hearts and to speak a few words of disrespect, these five hundred people had to be beggars for five hundred lifetimes, enduring a lot of hardship, suffering, hunger, cold and degradation from a lot of other people because of their position and their life style. Then even after they had paid all their retribution for their sins, met the Buddha, and become sangha members, even then, a little bit of residue of this disrespect karma from their past life still lingered around the atmosphere of their surroundings. That was why Prince Victorious, out of nowhere, still smelled it, still could taste it, could see it, could feel it with his intuition. That was why he reacted like he did, not wanting to invite them to his banquet of offering.

So actually, whatever we did or we do, even though no one knows it, even though those persons have never seen us doing these things before or have never met us even, they would still be able to detect something from our aura, from our energy field, our magnetic field, and then react accordingly. That's why we must take care all the time to keep ourselves impeccably pure, clean, and consciously strive to keep it always like this. Otherwise, whatever happens to us, we cannot blame anyone else.

104

# Princess Forbearance

This is another Buddhist story. It is called the Chun-ren Princess. Chun means pure, ren means patient. Because this person was very good at being patient, she was called Chun-ren.

This princess was the youngest daughter of a king whose name was Bersna. This princess was very filial to her parents and had a lot of patience. But she had one defect, which was that she was very ugly, too ugly, terribly ugly, incredibly ugly. (Laughter) Because of this, she did not get married even by the time she was eighteen years old. This "flower" had been in bloom for a long time. (Laughter)

Her parents could never arrange their daughter's marriage. They tried to find a husband for her but all was in vain. They blamed God for being unfair, saying that Hes was so careless for giving her such a face. This princess was so ugly that whoever saw her could not endure it, and would lose their nerve.

How ugly was she? Oh! Her nose was so low and flat and her two nostrils were big and pointed upwards to the sky! (Master and everyone laugh.) Everyone would see her two nostrils immediately. Her forehead was bumpy. Her teeth grew outwards, just as if they did not want to help her keep any secret. (Laughter) All her teeth were going out for some fresh air. They were too hot to stay in her mouth. Her eyes didn't look like eyes, they were too big and awful.

I have not mentioned her figure yet. (Laughter) She was tall and slender. But it didn't match. She walked like a scarecrow. Whoever saw her would think they had just encountered a ghost. It was horrible! So many young royal men went to study abroad as an excuse to stay away. (Master and everyone laugh.) The story says that they were afraid to be her husband!

That princess grieved and regretted deeply when she watched her two sisters as they looked in the mirror and were happy with their appearance. She was never jealous of her sisters, she was just sad and regretful of her own situation. She was a lady of high spirit and virtue, but her sisters were proud of themselves, and no one liked them. She was different. Although she was ugly, everyone liked her a lot.

Her sisters were arrogant and proud of their beauty. They knew their sister was very ugly, so they intentionally moved their eyes around (laughter) to ignore her. They looked at her with unfriendly eyes, and even turned their bottoms up at her. (Laughter) They never looked at her with an attitude of friendship or closeness, never chatted with her, never said hello to her, never comforted her, and never had any contact with her at all. They even told the king to never let her go out of the palace to avoid someone speaking ill of them or despising the royalty. Since then she wasn't allowed to play outside.

Without any friends, she was lonely and felt stressful. However, even in that situation, she was still filial to her parents and respected her sisters. She treated subordinates and servants very considerately and generously. When someone was short of something or when poor people needed help, she would try her best to help them. She handed out her own treasures and pocket money to purchase medicine for the needy. If someone was sick she tried to take care of him or her, or she would ask a doctor to care for him or her. That was why everyone liked her very much, but they didn't like her two sisters. Her reputation for meritorious deeds, despite her unpleasant appearance, spread all over the country, even to the neighboring country. Both her virtue and appearance were well-known.

One day the neighboring country's prince, whose name was Chun-der (in Chinese the name means caring about merits), came to the kingdom. Maybe he did not care about feminine charm because Prince Chun-der wanted to marry her. Well! All of the people in the palace were shocked! The king held the prince's hands the whole time, worried that he might change his mind. (Master and everyone laugh.) The king made the excuse that he was thanking him, but actually he was worried that the prince might run away. The king grasped the prince's hands and called him I-chie ("I-chie" in Chinese means a person with a sense of justice).

The king said to Chun-der, "I am appreciative of your love for my daughter. No language can express my feelings. You are an I-chie, you care for merits more than feminine charm! If you need anything in the future, I will support you completely. From now on, both our countries will live and die together," et cetera.

The king still advised the prince to keep his daughter inside after the marriage, not let her leave the palace, (laughter) to avoid people's gossip.

The prince escorted her home, and did what the king said. Although the prince's mind was very open and very generous, his capacity was still limited. The princess' ugly appearance, however, was unlimited. The limited versus the unlimited.

Finally the prince could not stand it anymore. Even though sometimes he admired her virtues, when he looked at her, he couldn't bear it anymore, not even one more glance. Gradually, Chun-der began to enjoy playing and having fun more than caring about merits. He went out, giving all kinds of excuses. He went hunting, drinking, playing chess, et cetera. He did not see her often.

The princess lived in the palace and had everything, but she was just like a bird. She was put in a golden cage of depression. She was always within the walls, and so did not know what was happening on the outside. The princess was very melancholy, but she believed that was her fate. She was very patient. She always thought about the cause of her current situation. Maybe it was due to her lack of spiritual practice in past lives, or due to heavy karma. But she did her duty well and never complained. She always treated her husband the same as the first day they were together. She bore lots of disdain but was very loyal, took good care of him, and heartily supported him. Even though she treated people in the palace very generously, some unhappy events still occurred.

The king's concubines, princesses and the royal family relatives came to show off their beauties. They even talked about her ugly appearance in public. The princess was a really tolerant person. She continuously endured all this and never got angry. She never treated people impolitely. She was always well mannered, patient and gentle.

One day those vicious royal ladies and princesses thought of a trick to tease her. They asked their husbands to hold a banquet and to invite everyone, including the prince and his wife. Usually this kind of dance party required the husband and wife to come as a couple. These ladies were of the same age as the prince, and were very haughty.

Finally Prince Chun-der just came alone. Those royal ladies and princesses, those who were married and those who were single, all showed off to the prince and teased him. They tried to flirt and attract him, et cetera. Sometimes they teased him purposely and tried to make him feel sad, knowing that his wife was very ugly.

The prince no longer cared about the merits. He could not bear the teasing any longer. He became mad at his wife. He ran back home in anger and shame. He told himself that he had to divorce her. He just couldn't stand it anymore.

On the same day, but before her husband returned home,

the princess was alone in her room, not knowing what was happening. Suddenly she felt frightened and terrible inside. It was as
if her sixth sense was telling her something bad was about to
happen. At home, the princess thought about herself and shed
tears. She cried alone. Her body and appearance were strange,
which gave her much pain. She clasped both hands in salutation
and kneeled. She prayed to the living Buddha, who was Shakyamuni
at that time. She was probably the Buddha's disciple or she may
have just heard of Buddha's name.

She prayed, "You are the living Buddha who rescues people
from suffering and obstacles. I am the most suffering person now.
I can't leave home to pay my respect to You, so please know my
wish and come to see me. Understand that my desire is for You to
be here."

Shakyamuni Buddha sensed her sincerity at his Jetavana
Monastery and flew over with His transformation body. The prin-
cess burst into
tears when she
saw Buddha!
She was joyful
and sad, and
kept crying.
She told
Shakyamuni
Buddha, "My
respect to Buddha.
I don't know what my
previous life was!"
The princess
asked Buddha if she could know what

karma she had created in her past lives to make her body and appearance so strange; and what good deeds she had done so that she was born in a rich and respectable family. People respected her and some envied her, but some would joke and discriminate against her due to her appearance. She repented her bad deeds in front of Buddha. She asked Buddha to believe her sincerity. She regretted her past karma if there was any.

The Buddha told her, "In your previous life, you were a beautiful wife, a beautiful lady. However, you were very cold-hearted towards your servants and you were jealous of your friends and relatives who were beautiful. You would stare at those who had more beauty. You treated people unkindly. Relying on your good looks, you showed no respect to others. You were arrogant and rude. If you repent very sincerely now, this karma will be gone with an open mind, because everything is created by the mind."

The princess heard the voice of the transformation body of the Buddha. The voice she heard was so soft, beautiful and warm. She felt so happy, bright and comfortable. She repented more deeply. She kneeled there and asked Buddha to help her resolve her karma. Because she was very sincere and repented wholeheartedly, Shakyamuni Buddha's transformation body touched her head. Then she looked at His eyes.

It says that she kept looking for a long time. (Laughter) Maybe she was in samadhi, so it lasted a long time. It says for even several hours. As she looked at Shakyamuni Buddha's eyes, her eyes became very pretty and shiny, like His. When she looked at the dignified appearance of the Buddha, suddenly her appearance became dignified and beautiful. She felt very happy. The most joyous feelings came over her. She admired, respected, and loved the Buddha very much.

At whatever part of the Buddha she looked, her body changed too; and immediately she became a very beautiful princess. After Shakyamuni Buddha had transformed Himself to speak to her, He flew away using magical power. It says that He used magical power but this was His transformation body!

The Buddha was gone. Then the prince came back home. At that time, he could not endure anymore and wanted a divorce. When the princess heard the sound of galloping at full speed, her heart beat faster as she thought something might happen. She was so nervous when going out to meet her husband.

She saw that her husband was full of viciousness and also looked like he was in a bad mood, so she dared not say anything. Instead she kneeled down and took off his shoes. She did the same as usual whenever her husband came home. She helped him take off his shoes to make him feel comfortable. She massaged his feet. Then she removed his crown because it was very heavy. This was how this wife routinely treated her husband. She put the sword back into its place, and then removed his waist belt, which was completely decorated with pearls and agates and was also very heavy.

Ah, then the prince saw her. He wondered who she was and looked around at her. "No, it's not her!" But the person who had that kind of behavior should be his wife, the princess. She did the same job, in the same manner and with the same attitude; but the face was different, and the figure too! He looked around and wondered why. He asked the princess, "Who are you?"

The princess understood his confusion and then told the whole story about seeing Buddha, and how she changed, et cetera. Wow! He was too happy to want to divorce her! (Laughter) Later, he knew that to practice meditation was the greatest blessing, so they meditated together. (Laughter) Maybe they went to have initiation and attended group meditation on that day. They became very diligent in practicing for merits and blessings, in giving charity and meditating for wisdom.

One day, since both of them were in a good mood, they

just chatted with each other. The princess could not control herself and told her husband, "I think you care more about feminine charm than merits." (Laughter)

She wanted to change his name because the prince desired feminine charm more than merits. The prince was embarrassed, so he skipped to another subject to talk about other things. (Laughter)

For the princess, her time had come, so she was stuck in this compelling situation. She even could not go out to worship Buddha. She was longing for Buddha, not longing for beauty. She was really longing for Buddha because she said she didn't have a good fate, and her body and appearance were so terrible that she didn't even have freedom. She was a noble princess, but she had no freedom. All the people around her criticized her; criticized her so much that it cleansed her karma! That day, even her respected husband wanted to divorce her, and mistreated her. But all this suffering cleansed some of her karma.

This made her feel very depressed and hurt – not being allowed to see the Buddha – even though she was so eager to see Him. So she prayed for Him to come, to let her have a look. She did not hope for any change in her appearance. She did not intend to ask Buddha for any help, she only repented because she knew it was the karma of her previous life. She was changed by such a situation.

What I mean is, practitioners don't need to ask for these material things. If they come, they come naturally; and it doesn't matter if nothing happens. The most important thing is to seek the Truth sincerely, to take care of our virtues, then external things will be good naturally. Just like Jesus said, *Seek you first the Kingdom of God, then all other things shall be added unto you.*

We should be confident that we are more beautiful. Don't

you think you are beautiful, so light and bright? Yes. Our inner beauty comes out. When other people see us, they would think we are beautiful. Sometimes it happens this way. They are blinded by our inner bright quality, so they cannot see our weaknesses, and our outer appearance. That's true.

When we are joyful, happy and open minded, don't we look beautiful? (Audience: Yes.) Some look nice and beautiful but they have a sad face, so we don't want to see them. No matter how beautiful you are, I would not look at those sad faces even if you begged me to do so. You don't need to care for your outer appearance too much, only for what's inside. If we are beautiful inside, the outside should be the same. The negative power that comes out from the inside makes the outside dark.

When we are sad, we look ugly. We practitioners don't long for things outside, but they will come to us naturally. If we don't have those things, we are still okay. After practicing more, we don't even care about those things. Physical beauty is good, but not being physically beautiful is also good.

# A **Stingy** Old Woman

At the foot of a mountain in India, there lived an old woman. This woman, she loved "seclusion". Most people when they love seclusion, it means they want to be one with God, they want to be alone so that they can think of God, they can meditate on God, they can remember God, they can love God, they can see God, they can hear God, they can talk to God, et cetera. That is true seclusion.

But for this woman, it was not the case. She was the worst of all the misers in the country, means she was very stingy. She lived alone in seclusion just because she didn't like to share her possessions, her food with other people. Charity was unknown to her. She would not part with even one grain of rice for the Cambodian people. (Laughter) During her lifetime, never ever did she give anything at all, not even her old cleaning mop. When it was worn out, she would repair it, keep it somewhere in case, and never give it to anyone.

Now, there is a God called Lord Vishnu; you know Vishnu, second world God. He watched with interest the life and actions of this famous old lady. He found that she was to die soon, after New Years. (Laughter) After she eats the first rice cake, she's probably going to choke to death. Actually, there are many old Japanese people who choke on rice cakes during the New Year's festival. Make sure you don't eat too many rice cakes, the sticky rice cake? I don't know how they can choke on it, but actually someone did.

The Lord saw that she had only three more days of her life on Earth. (How good! So people can share some of her possessions after she's gone.) The Lord, therefore, called Busandi to his side and said to him, "My very dearly beloved Busandi, snatch something from her at least today, because tomorrow she has to die. When she dies, she will have some merit to her credit if you steal something from her, at least some chocolate, or maybe popcorn." (Laughter)

Busandi nodded okay; and taking the form of a crow, he sat on the tree near the house of Kachani. Kachani was the old woman's name. It was the time when she was washing a handful of black gram, soaking it in water to cook for her food. Now, Busandi decided to snatch away a beak full of it. Suddenly, in one leap, he flew near the vessel and took a mouthful of grain with lightning speed, "Chi!" (Laughter)

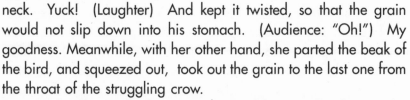

But, the alert old woman grabbed him with greater speed still, grabbed him by the neck like this. She wrung his neck. Yuck! (Laughter) And kept it twisted, so that the grain would not slip down into his stomach. (Audience: "Oh!") My goodness. Meanwhile, with her other hand, she parted the beak of the bird, and squeezed out, took out the grain to the last one from the throat of the struggling crow.

Oh! This really deserves an award from us (laughter) – The Most Miserly Woman In History. I don't know if there was such a story, there must have been. Some people are so stingy, stupid, cruel and cold blooded. Busandi struggled for his life, gulp, gulp, gulp... (Laughter) At last, he was let free after she thought all the grain had been poked out by her.

He flew to Lord Vishnu and fell at his feet, half dead. Lord Vishnu questioned him as to what had happened after he left him. Busandi gasped out the whole story. Pantingly he said, "Oh Lord, I was almost strangled to death. I could not succeed in my mission, I'm very sorry. I could not get even a grain of food from that wretched old woman."

Then the Lord said, "Oh, Busandi, do not say so. Come, let me examine in your mouth. (Laughter) Open your mouth, let

me have a look.

So Busandi opened his beak, and Lord Vishnu used his wisdom eye with a magnifying glass to look into his throat, "Ah, there is something there. (Laughter) What is it? Let me see what it is, must be something."

He saw a little bit of husk, the outer skin, shell of the grain, sticking to his palate. (Laughter) Thank God! At least he did not waste his time and struggle for nothing. "Look, Busandi, there's a small bit of husk sticking to your palate. I am satisfied," the Lord said.

Oh! the Lord is easy to satisfy.

So now, the old lady had earned some merit. Oh, blessed be the Lord, so compassionate, loving and merciful! Now he said, "Busandi, when she goes back to the world after her death, let her be fed on the husk of the particular grain which was found sticking to your palate."

The old woman will be eating that all her life long. The Lord so saying, disappeared.

Great and marvelous are the benefits of charity and righteousness, even involuntarily. Infinite and overwhelming is the love and compassion of the Lord. Such is the mysterious potency of even the least act of kindness and charity. Probably she didn't want to take it out because she knew it was useless. "Ah, there's not much there." (Laughter)

The Lord himself, in his great love, creates opportunities for the redemption and deification of the sinning human beings. The old woman who did no meritorious act was ordained to get bread made of husk. And if we gave people a lot more, how much would we have?

# Three
# *STUBBORN*
## Servants

**A** rich man, a billionaire, had three servants. One was very thoughtful, one was very prudent, and the other one was very polite. The rich man was very pleased with and liked them very much.

One time, the son of the rich man fell into a river by accident and was drowning. The second servant, who was very prudent, saw this. However he was so prudent that he went back to tell his master, "Master, your son just fell into the river. May I save him? (Audience laughs.) Do you think we can save him or not? What's the best way? Both of us must discuss it."

Of course, the rich man was very angry and threw him out.

By the time the rich man ran to save his son, it was too late. So he ordered the first servant, who was very thoughtful, to buy a coffin to bury his son. Since this servant was a person who prepared for things that had not yet happened, he bought two coffins. (Master and audience laugh.) He was too thoughtful! His master was so angry and said, "Only one son died, why have you bought two coffins?"

The servant replied, "In case your second son dies, maybe drowns or has any other kind of accident, (audience laughs) we don't need to buy again. Saves trouble, saves time, saves gasoline!"

That rich man was extremely angry and threw him out!

Now there was just one servant left. The one who was very polite. The rich man was still very pleased with him. One day, he and another servant went out sightseeing with their master, carrying him in a sedan. On the way, they came to a swampy river where the water was not very deep. If they crossed the water, their clothes would get dirty and wet. The other servant hesitated. He didn't want to dirty his clothes, and so wanted to return home. However, the polite servant said, "Don't go back! As long as our master is happy, we should go ahead. We, ourselves, are not important."

Then they crossed the water without caring about themselves.

When the master heard that his servant was so loyal to him, he was very happy. He then said to the servant, "Since you are so thoughtful, so devoted and so faithful to me, I will give you many new clothes and raise your salary when we return home."

As soon as the polite servant heard that, he put down the sedan (at that very moment, they were standing in the middle of the river), and answered with his palms together, "Thank you for your goodness, master!" (Master and audience laugh.)

You see, there is not much difference comparing them to our initiates, is there? (Audience laughs.) They don't know how to evaluate the situation and act accordingly. Everyone has his own attribute, but uses it in the wrong place.

You remember that Confucius had many well-known disciples. Tze-Lu was very brave and Zan-Chio was very prudent. But each one only had that quality. If you are too prudent, you wouldn't know how to relax. If you are too brave, you wouldn't know when to be humble. So we know that it is not good to be an extremist.

Although they were very good, they still came to learn from Confucius because he embodied all the qualities – brave but not too brave, humble but not too humble. He knew how to behave under any circumstances. He handled everything in a neutral manner and not too fanatically.

Most of us have a stiff-necked quality. If we use it in the right place, it would be good. However, if we use it in the wrong place, it would be bad. Just like we can use electricity to light up a bulb, or to make cold or hot air; but if we touch the electricity directly, we would be in trouble. Also, there are many newly-invented remedies that can cure people; but an overdose would be harmful.

We come to this world to learn how to be perfect, so we should have every quality and know how to use them appropriately. We can not say that because we are very brave, then we can go ahead and do things without caring about anything. If we are brave but have no wisdom, we can hurt ourselves and others.

# Recover

# Our

# Humility

**A** person wanted very much to pursue spiritual practice. He read many stories and scriptures, and all of them said: "Humility is the prime quality showing that someone has attained sainthood."

Therefore, he longed to learn to be humble.

He followed a master to study. He told his master that he longed to see God, but he didn't know how he could learn to be humble. He felt himself to be unclean, impure and not humble, so he could not see God.

His master said, "Good! Now you go and find someone or something filthier, lower and more inferior than you. Bring it to me, or just tell me. Then I can teach you how to learn from it, how to become humbler."

He went from Taipei to Kaohsiung but failed to find anyone, not even in Miaoli. Though we are so lousy, he couldn't find anyone lousier than himself. He felt frustrated.

Once, when in the toilet, he suddenly thought that the feces must be filthier and lower than himself, since no one would want it and would run away covering their noses upon seeing it. He wanted to take a heap of feces to his master, because he could not find anything lower than that.

Just as he reached out his hand, and before he touched "it," he suddenly heard a voice say, "Don't touch me! Don't move! Don't touch me!"

The man was amazed and wondered who was talking. Then the voice was heard again, "Don't you touch me!"

It seemed that the feces was talking to him. Totally bewildered, he asked, "Why not? Why can't I touch you?"

It said, "Don't you see? I was a perfect piece of cake yesterday. (Audience laughs.) I was so pretty, so valuable and precious, that I was fit to be consumed by a king, or to be offered to a great saint. Now, just because of having associated with you once, today I have been transformed into this state. No one wants to see me now, not even get close. When they see me, they close their eyes, block their noses, and run away quickly. Everyone despises me. I turned into this state just because I associated with you once! If you touch me once more, oh terrible, (audience laughs) who knows what I will become? I don't know what more terrible things will happen to me. So, please don't touch me anymore."

Then, the man really understood and felt humble.

We all think we are very good, but the truth is that we might not be! We think we are better than the feces, but the truth is that it turned into that state because of us. We spiritual practitioners know very well whether we have the quality of humility or not. Don't think that we are anything great.

The Red Goblin
And
The Green Goblin

There is a story about two demighosts, demigods; perhaps, half angel and half goblin-like. They lived together, the two. One was green and the other red, (Master laughs) just like the green light and red light outside. Green is for peaceful, smooth going. Red is for war, stop, obstruction. But both of them lived happily together in the mountain with no problems, no anxieties, no desires, nothing.

They lived there for many, many hundreds of years already. And often when they had nothing to do, they would sit on top of the mountain and look down into the world below them, the world of humankind. They saw all the busyness, the people walking up and down, and all that. They saw the world was always changing. So the green said to the red, "You see, we have lived here many hundreds of years already and our life has never changed, every day the same thing. But the world below, the world of human beings, every day change. How come?"

The red said, "Oh, yes, you're right, very interesting. Their life is more interesting."

But the green said, "Why is it that their life is so changing all the time?"

Then the red thought for a while and said, "Oh, it must be because they are always fighting with each other. They build a building, beautiful and big, and the next day, they fight and demolished it. Then they build another one, have a war, and destroy it again. That's why the world always has something to do. (Master laughs.) That's why the world is always changing. So now in our world here, for the two of us, it's too peaceful, too boring. I think we ought to start fighting with each other."

That's what the red thought.

The green said, "No! No fighting. We are good friends, we've been friends for many hundreds of years. How can we fight each other?"

But the red said, "If we don't fight, then we can't have any change. Our life will always go on like this. It's boring and we don't make any progress. So let's fight!"

The green said, "No, no, no! I can not do it. No, we are friends."

The red insisted and said, "From today you are my enemy. That's it."

He declared war right there, and then left. He didn't live with the green anymore. He moved to the other side of the mountain and sat there alone, prepared for war. The green stayed there in that corner of the mountain, feeling so lonely and miserable. He missed the other goblin.

Goblins, kind of demiangels, have magical power. Apart from being able to fly, making things appear by themselves, seeing very far, hearing very far, they also have a long nose which can stretch to no limit.

The green goblin sat there one day feeling very bored. Suddenly, he noticed in the world of humans below that something was flashing, shining all the time. So he was curious and used his nose. (Laughter) He made his nose long. He said, "Grow longer, grow longer, grow longer."

Then his nose kept growing long, long, long, piercing into the world below where the shining and flashing was happening. The shining and flashing came from the clothes of the princess of that city. It happened that the servants were hanging her clothes outside to air them. They had gold flakes on them and also some were studded with diamonds, rubies, et cetera. So they glittered in the sun, and that's why they were shining and flashing.

Now the servants said to each other, "Oh, her clothes are so beautiful, but so many. We don't have enough bamboo poles to hang them on. What to do?"

At that moment, the nose of the goblin just arrived in time. (Laughter) The servants thought, "Oh, we have a bamboo pole long enough to hang the rest of the clothes on."

So they put the rest of the clothes of the princess on this green pole, then happily went inside to eat some chapatis.

The green goblin suddenly felt something so heavy on his nose. He got scared. He immediately pulled his nose back to the normal size and there with it came a bundle of glittering clothes at his feet. He thought, "Ah, oh, it must be a lucky day."

So he tried them on to see how beautifully they looked! He was proud, marching around all by himself.

It happened that the red came over. He wanted to  start a fight, to progress. But then the green said, "Look here! I have some new clothes, beautiful; and I saved some, half of them, for you."

The red looked with contempt and said, "Look, I don't wear these kind of ridiculous things, only crazy people like you do."

He wanted to start a fight, so he talked nonsense.

The green was always green, he was very cool, he didn't pick on it. He said, "Okay, fine. If you don't wear them, it doesn't harm anything. Leave them there. It's all right."

The red didn't know what else to do, so he went home. Actually he was very, very jealous of the green and later he tried to get some clothes for himself. He also put his nose very long down into the palace, waiting for some clothes to be hung on it. But it happened that the samurai, at that time, were practicing sword together. When they saw such a long thing coming, they said to each other, "What's that?"

One said, "Ah, it must be a new invention of the enemy trying to attack us. Let's destroy it first."

"Oh, okay," said the other.

Then "pa" (Master imitates the sound of cutting) with the sword. Suddenly the red felt such a sharp pain. Immediately he pulled back his nose to the normal size. It was bleeding; he cried and cried so much.

The green heard his crying, came over, and said, "What happened, what happened?"

The red was so embarrassed, angry and could not say what the truth was, so he said, "Leave me alone. Don't bother me."

The green said, "No, I won't bother you, I'm trying to help you. It's bleeding. Look here, I know the medicine. I'll put it on. It will stop right away and your nose will become beautiful like before. Otherwise, you will have a big scar, a big hole there. Then it will be very ugly. I just want to take care of you."

The red, after all, felt touched and said, "All right, all right." Then he cried his heart out, "Ah, it really hurts. Please quickly, quickly. Make it better, quickly."

Of course, they made peace together because he had enough with fighting. He thought fighting was no good. He learned the lesson of peace. From then on, they wore nice clothes, drank tea together every day, and no more war.

# The Magical

## *Chair*

Long ago there was an old man. He lived at the foot of a mountain and was very poor. His straw hut was his only possession. In fact, this person was very lazy, so he deserved it!

One day, he heard that in a certain place there lived a very powerful yogi who had the supernatural power to create anything he desired. After hearing this, the very lazy person, who did not want to work, wished to go there to ask the yogi to use his supernatural power to create things for him, so that he would not have to work anymore. After thinking in this way, he left.

He walked a very long way to the mountain cave where the yogi lived. When he saw the yogi, he prostrated. The yogi was quite nice, he politely entertained him and asked him about his purpose. The lazy man said, "Respected and beloved master, I am a very poor person. Besides a small straw hut, I have nothing else. Now I am very old and not able to work, so please, compassionate master, please help me.

Grant me some possessions to live on. I know you have a lot of supernatural power. You can immediately create anything you desire. I believe you are able to help me."

That yogi closed his eyes and sat there quietly without saying a word. Perhaps he was too tired listening to all of this. The old man then continued to ask him. After making requests for a long time, this yogi reluctantly gave him a chair and said, "After you go home, anytime you think of something you want, you can sit on this chair. You have to wash your hands, face and take a bath before sitting on the chair. Then think about anything you desire. This way you will surely get it."

After thanking the yogi, the old man took the chair and immediately rushed home! Reaching home, he did not waste a bit of time. He immediately washed his hands, face, took a bath; then he sat on the chair right away. At that time he was very hungry, so he immediately thought about food. Food immediately appeared. Oh! Very beautiful, very nice and a very bountiful meal. He enjoyed all the good food until he was very full.

After eating he felt tired and desired a bed to rest. Immediately a bed with a thick mattress appeared. He layed down to sleep, but he could not really rest because in his heart, he was always thinking of wanting things and money. He jumped up from the bed and sat on the chair. Now he started to think about transforming his straw hut into a palace. As he was thinking this, the straw hut immediately disappeared!

This old man's palace was very, very beautiful with jewels all over. The doors were made of gold. The floors and the ceilings were made with gold, even the pillars were of gold inlaid with jewels, very precious. Thus he was very happy and felt very comfortable. He continued to think, "Ah! Such a big palace should not be without any servants."

He just thought and many servants appeared waiting for

his commands. Later he thought, "The servants, the palace can not be without money!"

He thought of a lot of gold, silver and money. Suddenly all these appeared together. It made this old man very happy indeed. But he suddenly became worried. He thought, "Ah! My palace is so beautiful, with so many possessions, if it happened that an earthquake should come, what to do?" (Master and all laugh.)

He just finished the thought and an earthquake came. (Master laughs.) His possessions and the palace were squashed into the earth.

What does this story tell us? Our mind has to be clean and pure first. It is not good enough having supernatural power or power of practice. Therefore, we have to clean our body, speech and thoughts before having the power. If we have the power but our body, speech and mind are not clean, precepts are not kept properly, then we could do bad things. Our own power could hurt ourselves. Sometimes this power could hurt others. Thus since ancient times, those masters, before taking any disciple, would test the disciple for a long time until his body, speech and mind were completely clean before giving him the power.

Master often tells you not to practice supernatural power. The ordinary people outside can practice supernatural power easily. They do not have to keep any precepts and do not have to be vegetarian. When we still cannot control our mind, if we think about bad things, they appear at once; because at that time, we get whatever we think. The power in the universe is immense, but we should know how to use it. Otherwise, it can cause a lot of harm, harming ourselves and damaging the world.

Some disasters we see in the world are sometimes not necessarily the karma of the people, but due to some people who practice supernatural power. They practice towards the bad direction; or because of their messed-up thinking, they then mess up the world. We can say that these people created trouble or were possessed by the negative power. Really there are such people.

Thus when we practice, we have to think about God every day, think about those fully charged names of the Buddhas to protect ourselves. Sometimes it is not entirely our own karma that causes our obstructions, but the negative, maya power around us that affects us. Thinking a lot about God Almighty, our mind becomes clean and then we do not desire anything. To us, at that time, supernatural power would be of no use, because we would be one with God and there would be nothing we could not have.

At that time, we would be very satisfied inside and we would know that after we have left this illusive world, we would go back to our Homeland where we would have everything. Compared to that place, this world is junk. Nothing could possibly tempt us. After our soul has returned many times to the Homeland to take a look, our mind would understand and would be very stable. Then we would not want anything. Even if we did want, we would only want those things that are good for others. Our heart would be very kind, always thinking of positive things. Once thinking about the positive things, then the positive things would come.

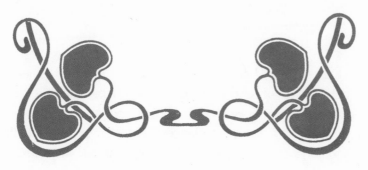

# $O$ur

# Faith In God

$T$here was a person who had a car accident. He was ejected out of the car and hung dangling on the branches of a tree. He was in danger. He had never believed in God before and he never recited the name of Suma Ching Hai or anything like that. (Laughter) So, at that dangerous moment that he called out for help, no one was around.

"Oh God, at least You are there, no? I have never prayed to You before, but today I am praying. Please come and help me. Please!"

Nothing happened. God didn't say anything or maybe Hes wasn't there.

So he continued again, "Oh God, please don't be angry with me. I know I never called You during my life, but at least I am calling You today. I believe in You, don't I? That is why I am calling You, no? If I didn't believe in You, how would I call You? Please come quickly and help me."

Nothing happened. God didn't say anything.

He nearly dropped down the cliff because he was very tired. The cliff was loosening so he said, "Oh God, please come quickly! I promise You I will spread Your name all over the continent. I will become a priest; I will preach, all over, the doctrine of God. I will tell everyone to believe in You, because if You save me today, I am the witness. I will tell them of this miracle and then I am sure everyone will run after You. I promise I will be Your priest, Your servant, anything You want."

So there came a voice from somewhere, "Everyone says that when they are in trouble."

Then the person said, "Oh no God, not me, not me. I really believe in You. If You help me, I really will. I promise."

God, the voice, said, "Alright I'll give you a chance. Now, let go of that branch, and then I will save you."

The person said, "What!? Do you think I'm crazy?"

That's how he believed in God.

This sounds very similar to some of our initiates, "I believe in the Master, but what? You tell me to do that. What for?"

# We Should Not Copy A Master's

# *Outer Performance*

There was a master who trained his disciples in wisdom. Some came to the master and wanted to be trained in wisdom. So he said, "Yeah, of course to be a future master, future Buddha, we must be endowed with at least two gifts. There are many important qualities for a future Buddha but there are two important gifts that one must have in order to advance quickly in spiritual practice."

So the disciples asked him, "What are they? What are these two gifts?"

The master said, "The first is the power of endurance. Endurance means you endure anything that other people cannot. The second is the power of observation – look, look, look."

To demonstrate, the master immediately told the attendant to bring in a bowl with a lot of filthy things inside, that once you even smelled it you'd want to vomit. But the master was very unmoved. He put his finger inside the bowl of very filthy, disgusting things; full of the things that you wouldn't even want to look at – maybe straight from the restroom. He put his finger inside, then took his hand and put his finger in his mouth. His face didn't move, just like the wall in front of you or me.

The future Buddhas surrounding him were very eager to try to show the master that they were qualified to be his disciples. So all of them came, put their finger in the bowl, then put it in their mouths, and managed not to move their faces. No expression of disgust or anything.

The master laughed and said, "Congratulations, you have passed one test but not two. The one test that you really passed was the test of endurance. But the second test you failed because you didn't have the power of observation."

The disciples said, "Why?"

The master then said, "I put this finger in but I put the other finger in my mouth."

He put the index finger in the filthy bowl but he put the middle finger in his mouth. (Laughter) The disciples didn't see anything. They put the same finger in the bowl as they put in their mouths.

So you see what it is now. Those are stupid disciples. That's the way of many of the disciples. They just copycat the master. Copy anything, anything, anything; then they make a fool of themselves. That's the trouble. So we don't copy anyone. Even the master wouldn't copy anyone. If we want to be like the master, then we don't copy anyone. Everything is original because each one is endowed with the power of creativity. Everyone can create everything, according to his and her ability and artistic tendency.

We don't have to copy anyone, including the Buddha, the master or the Patriarch of the whole world. That is why you see many masters, they don't look like the others. The Patriarch Hue Neng didn't look like the Buddha and didn't act like the Buddha. Jesus didn't act the same as Lao Tze. Lao Tze again didn't do anything that resembled Krishna, et cetera. So if we copy the master, or we expect the master to look like the one that we read about in the Bible or the one we have imagined in our head, then we never can find a master. We shouldn't find the copy, we must find the original. The master is always original. We don't want a copy, do we?

So in our spiritual practice, we must always be vigilant. The master does things differently, sometimes very, very differently. We just look like that, and then we think we can do it – touch the head, looking in the eyes, give candy – candy we can buy, even more, things like that. It is not the outer performance from which you can judge whether that person is a master or not, it is something inside.

140

# Everything Is
# Created
# By The

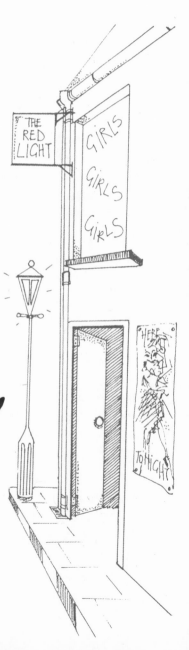

*Mind*

A long time ago, two friends took a trip together to visit and tour around. As they passed by an Indian temple, they heard someone reciting the Bhagavadgita inside. The Bhagavadgita is a very famous sutra in India. One of the friends said to the other, "Come on! Let's go inside to listen to the sutra."

So both of them went inside. However, only one stayed to listen, and the other took one glimpse and went out to look for girls in a brothel.

The one that went to a brothel soon felt bored. He regretted what he had done and felt quite ashamed. He thought, "Gosh! This is really nonsense! I am so ashamed. Why did I come to such a place instead of listening to the holy teachings? My friend is listening to the sutra now and receiving boundless merits while I've degraded myself at a place of prostitutes. How demoralizing!"

He felt disgusted and ashamed with himself, so he went back to the temple to listen to the sutra. However, when he arrived there, it was already over. He was truly sorry and repented for several days afterwards.

While he was feeling ashamed at the brothel, his friend in the temple was unable to calm his mind to listen to the sutra. (Master laughs.) His mind kept wondering to the brothel and thought, "Gosh! This is really boring! Why do I continue to stay here listening to the sutra? My friend is now eating and drinking and having a good time, while I sit here listening to some sutra. How boring!" (Master laughs.)

As he thought about it, he got into a bad mood.

After a long time, both of the friends died. The angel of death pulled the friend who listened to the sutra to hell, and dragged the friend who went to the brothel to heaven. (Master laughs.)

Do you know why? It was because everything is created by the mind! God does not look at our conduct alone. Hes looks into our hearts! Sometimes, we see a person's behavior but we don't really know if he is that way. Unless we can measure from within, it is very difficult to judge the inner person. He may appear very kind, but his heart is not; or he may have a very loving heart, but it doesn't seem like that from his outer appearance.

The same with some of our fellow initiates. You know that they were not so virtuous in the past; some were big gangsters and some were lady gangsters. (Master and everyone laugh.) Some killed others or committed some deeds that were not acceptable by society. But after they repented, they tried to purify themselves and practiced self-cultivation sincerely. Eventually their sins will be cleansed.

Now there are some others who may not have committed any crime during their lifetime, but they just roam around, refuse to learn meditation, and take only half a glimpse at the Master and feel nothing. They leave to look for other masters. They are always 'shopping' around. We might say that they are "shopping around the mountains" because most of the enlightened masters live in the mountains. (Master laughs.) They jump from one mountain to another because the other seems greener and prettier. Due to their lack of sincerity in spiritual practice, they are not successful in the things they do.

Therefore, we cannot fool God by our seemingly kind outer appearance. We cannot fool God because to fool God means to fool ourselves. We are fully aware of what we want, and whatever we do. Whether we are sincere or not, we know it clearly.

You have also read some stories of the ancient masters. Some of them were pretty weird, like Jigong (a Chinese master).

We heard that he ate meat, drank wine, and was always drunk and falling down without dignity. Then there was the Chin-Shan living Buddha. He was also a weird monk. (Master laughs.) He was always very sloppy and undignified. But they practiced and knew their own level of spiritual attainment; and the Buddhas knew as well. Therefore, even though it is not easy to judge from the outside, as spiritual practitioners, we know from the inside whether we are sincere or not. Even if we don't know, God knows. It is not due to our outer performance that other people will believe in us, not necessarily so! God makes the judgement.

Being truly sincere is the most important in spiritual practice. At group meditation, some people may sit there quietly, but their minds are not focused. That's why Master often tells you that when you go to group meditation, you must keep your body, speech and mind clean. (Master laughs.) Otherwise, you receive no merit from sitting there; it is worse than those who meditate sincerely at home. They are very sincere and humble, as they meditated every day; thus, they receive more merit. (Master laughs.)

But of course, we will receive a lot of merit when we attend group meditation anyway, because the sincerity of the others will affect us. For example, when we come here and see hundreds and thousands of people meditating intently and sitting so seriously, we might feel ashamed and try to sit quietly for a while. (Master laughs.) Thus very naturally we will receive a lot of merit through concentration and the purification of the mind.

# Spiritual Practitioners Should *PROVIDE* For Themselves

There was a man who went into the deep forest, perhaps for sightseeing or to do some business. Then one day, he happened to see a fox who had lost all its legs. He wondered how the fox could survive in this jungle no longer having any legs. So he kept watching. Then he saw a tiger. It brought some game back and ate it. Whatever was leftover the fox fed himself on that. Now he knew, that's how it survived.

The next day again, God also fed the fox through the tiger. The man was thinking that he was somewhat enlightened now.

He said, "Ah, we have to depend on God. We must trust God, then Hes will provide everything for us."

So he dropped his business, forgot his wife and kids, and didn't even go to Hsihu Center for group meditation anymore. (Laughter) He just sat there in the forest, tried to surrender to God, and hoped that God would bring provisions to him. He sat there, meditating on God; and he didn't even recite the Holy Names or Namo the Supreme Master Ching Hai Wu Shang Shih Suma Tzu's name. (Laughter)

He said, "I just trust God. Why should I recite anyone's name? I trust God, I love God, I believe in God, I fear and respect God; that's enough for me. I surrender every-thing to God."

So he sat there. He waited for maybe butter and cakes, bread, cheese, tofu to arrive.

First day, nothing came, so he continued to sit there. He said, "God is testing my faith."

He sat there another day.

Second day, no tofu even appeared and no cabbage grew from the earth in front of his nose. Nothing happened, so he thought, "Oh, God must be testing my courage and my belief. Of course I'll show Hirm my faith, my surrender ability and my unwavering, unshaken trust in Hirm."

So he sat there again and kept waiting.

Third day came. Nothing happened – no butter, no bread, no cheese, no tofu, no cabbage, no carrots, not even water in the form of rain. Slurp, slurp. Now, he felt the test from his throat, his stomach, his limbs; not from God necessarily, but from all over his body. All the spare parts of his body began to try not to spare him. (Master and everyone laugh.) So he was suffering deeply and trying to think what had happened. He prayed to God, "Please don't test me any further, I truly trust You. I really surrender to You. My faith in You is unshaken. It can never die."

So there came a voice from heaven, or maybe from his stomach, I don't know. (Master and everyone laugh.) It said something like this, *"Oh, you stupid fool. Why do you learn the way of a disabled fox? Wake up. Walk the way of the tiger."*

Well, we can be monks too; but we should work, do some little thing for our living. That's why I told you we must earn our own bread, because we are provided with tools and intelligence. We are not disabled foxes. If we were, maybe God would provide for us. But since we are not disabled, why should we walk the way of a disabled animal? We should walk like a lion, tiger, elephant, horse. We should be the provider and not the beggar, not the receiver. That's the way of life. As long as we are still in this illusionary world, we should provide for ourselves; train ourselves; play with these tools, experiment with our ability and intelligence. Let's see what life has to offer. Let's see what tomorrow will bring.

With our intelligence and ability, we watch life growing inside us; we watch life changing with the seasons; we watch our tools bringing benefit to ourselves, our families and the society at large. We have intelligence, we should use it. Wisdom is one thing, intelligence and ability are another.

Wisdom we keep. Wisdom can never be taken away from us. Wisdom can never be trained, can never be defiled, can never be lessened or increased. Intelligence, knowledge, we should use, just to deal with daily life in this mundane world. Wisdom we can use it for a greater, more noble purpose like getting other people enlightened, or getting ourselves more power so that we can help those in need – like healing without healing, knowing without knowing, helping without helping, blessing the world without even a trace of arrogance, and without a trace of credit for our part. That's the way we should be.

So today, tomorrow or every day we meditate. This is just like walking the way of the tiger. We provide, we bless, we don't ask, we don't beg. I think God, the angels, enlightened beings are doing their part already. They are getting their job done. Now we have to follow their footsteps and do their job too – not always praying for ourselves or begging for this ephemeral life. Whenever we truly need something, we may pray for it. Just for that necessity so that we can go on with our spiritual life, but not forever being a beggar in the spiritual kingdom.

# The Method Of The Big **Boots**

In India, long time ago, there was a very nice, kind and good king. He loved his subjects very much. So he ruled with love, compassion and consideration for his people. But then, every time he saw one of them, he always noticed their feet. That was in the olden days, when people didn't have shoes yet, so their feet were always hurt by the stones and thorns. The thorns from the bushes would sometimes fall on the streets. So in walking all over, the thorns would stick into their feet. They would hurt, some-times bleed and get infected.

The king felt very, very heartbroken about this. He ordered his armies to get furs and the skins of the dead animals to spread on every road so that his subjects could walk on them and wouldn't get hurt. Not only the roads, but he ordered his people to put skins all over, on top of all of the earth of his country.

There was a very old and wise minister. He told the king that he had a better idea. He said, "Instead of spreading skins all over the earth, which is not convenient and would take a lot of time and money, you can just put them on each person's feet and then they can walk anywhere they want."

This sounds like a very funny story, but it just symbolizes something. Just like many people or ourselves, sometimes we want to make the world equal, peaceful, prosperous, friendly, loving, et cetera; but then it's not possible. Just like the thorns or stones, they will keep falling on the roads; sometimes even from the sky, on top of the earth. Doesn't matter how much you cover, there will always be stones and thorns falling back again, even on top of the skins. So, it is better that we just take care of our own feet.

The Quan Yin Method is just like the shoes for your feet. Even though the world is still full of problems, with thorns and stones, we can just walk over them, and we feel safe. As long as many people do not practice the Quan Yin Method, the world will still have problems. So if we want to be free from the trouble, we just protect our individual person. Then no problem. Perhaps problems still exist, but not so much for ourselves. You feel less and less affected by the troubles of the world. Sometimes if we do feel affected, it is because we have love, compassion for the ones who are affected.

# True Offering To God

This is a story about mental worship. Mental worship means a devotee, a follower doesn't use any external object such as flowers, incense, drums, gongs, statues or food offering, et cetera to worship.

You remember Arjuna, the devotee of Lord Krishna recounted in the Bhagavadgita? Arjuna was very fond of doing long and ostentatious external worship of God. He had a spacious worship room lit up with countless lights. He used gold and silver vessels. He spent several hours in ceremony and worship of Lord Shiva. He would sit for many hours and throw cart loads of flowers at the image of Lord Shiva. You know Lord Shiva, one of the Hindu Gods – Brahma, Vishnu and Shiva. Shiva is supposed to be the Lord of destruction. Actually he destroys evil, he doesn't destroy good persons.

There is a brother of Arjuna called Bhima. He never sat to do any worship. He never went to the temple. He always went to Miaoli. (Laughter, applause) He used to close his eyes for just a few minutes before dinner, and do mental worship of the Lord. Perhaps he made an offering, recited the Holy Names or something like that.

Arjuna thought that he was a great devotee of the Lord and that he was highly pious and devoted. He thought that his brother Bhima had no devotion. Therefore, he looked down upon him with contempt. (Laughter)

Lord Krishna found out the attitude of Arjuna, and wanted to teach him a good lesson to bring him to his senses. He proposed to Arjuna to take a trip to Mount Kailash, the abode of Lord Shiva.

When they were on their way, they met a man dragging a cart loaded with flowers of diverse kinds. Arjuna asked the man where he was taking the flowers, but the man kept silent as he was very much absorbed in his work, very concentrated. So Lord Krishna said to Arjuna, "Let us follow the man and find out the things for ourselves."

Arjuna agreed, and they both followed the man. They saw him empty the cart by the side of a huge heap of flowers, which was as big as the hill in Hsihu Center. They further saw several hundreds of carts, all loaded with flowers, approaching the same spot and their contents being emptied there. There was a huge mountain of fresh flowers there.

Arjuna became more and more curious. He could not control his curiosity anymore, so he asked the men, "Please tell me where these carts of flowers have come from."

None of them bothered to reply. But one man said after repeated questioning from Arjuna, "Venerable sir, kindly do not disturb us. We are too busy with our work. We have no time to talk to anyone. We have brought only seven hundred and fifty carts of flowers and more than seven hundred and fifty are still in the temple. They are all the flowers with which one Bhima, a son of Pandu, worshipped our Lord yesterday."

That means these mountains of flowers are only half of what they have to carry out, still half lay somewhere in the temple; and all these flowers came from Bhima, the brother of Arjuna, the lazy one, the one who never went to the temple, never worshipped the Lord, apparently, and never did anything, never gave a flower or incense to the Lord, the one that Arjuna always looked down upon as use- less, as atheist,

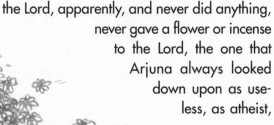

as not devoted to God.

"Now, it's hardly four more hours before his worship today and we must remove all the flowers within that time. Every day he worships, the mountain of flowers come."

So every day they have to remove so many flowers from his worship.

Arjuna was struck with wonder. He asked, "Is it Bhima or Arjuna that you speak of? Are you sure you have not made a mistake? You mean Arjuna, right? Arjuna, not Bhima!? My friend think, think about it. You're mistaken. The name is Arjuna, Arjuna, A-R-J-U-N-A. Must be!"

The man replied, "Poo! Don't talk about Arjuna. No, no, no! Not at all, not that one. It is Bhima who does such glorious worship with intense devotion, not his brother Arjuna, who merely makes an outward show of his worship."

Just then another man came with a basket of flowers. Lord Krishna asked that man, on purpose, not that he didn't know, "Ah, my friend, whose offering are these flowers?"

Of course you know the answer.

The man said, "They were offered yesterday by an ostentatious man who lives on the Earth. His name is Arjuna, (laughter) and he makes a display of his worship without any real love and devotion."

Therefore one basket of flowers and he talks so much about it.

Arjuna lowered his head in shame and said to the Lord, "Oh, Krishna, Ching Hai Wu Shang Shih, (laughter) why did you have to bring me here? Let us leave this place at once. You could have pointed it out — my de-

154

fects, my self-conceit, hypocrisy and ostentatiousness — at home, and saved all this trouble and exertion. I do admit that I thought very highly of my worship and devotion. I treated Bhima with contempt. Just now I realize that Bhima's short meditation with sincere devotion is more valuable than all my showy worship all day long."

Lord Krishna smiled and kept silent.

So you know in our place, in our non-temple temple, we don't bother with flowers, incense, drums, gongs or anything. We just bother with sincerity and inner devotion. That's why I tell you to concentrate and meditate, no need for outer performance so much, no need to even bow to me or bow to any Buddha.

If you see the Buddhas inside, you may bow to them if you want. But the Buddhas do not expect these things. They expect that you are devoted to yourself, so that you can find your inner nature and become Buddha or become one with God. Find your own glorious nature and be of help to yourself and many other beings. That is what the Buddha expects from us.

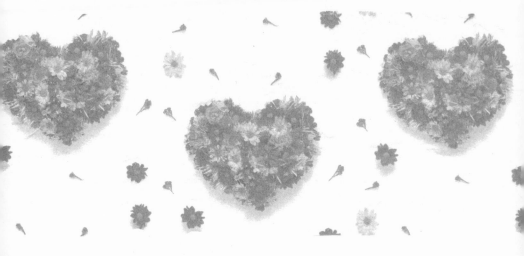

# The *Wisdom*

## Of An *Old*

## *Beggar*

## *Woman*

Most people who know don't talk, and the people who talk don't know. Of course those masters like Buddha or Jesus, they went and preached, but that was different. They had to do it. Otherwise, they wouldn't want to. Their mission was like that, even though they suffered. They didn't want it. But that didn't mean they'd always go out seeking the opportunity to debate. That is the difference. They would abhor and run away from such an opportunity. They just had to do the job, to teach the disciples, those who came to them. But they would not go out and argue with other people to show off their knowledge.

Now this Tiloba (Tiloba was the great, grand master of Milarepa's master) was one of those who ran around all India showing off his knowledge of books. Everywhere he went, he won. No one could ever win because his knowledge of books was so extensive. Well, in many countries we have these people, not only Tiloba.

One day he was in his house, reading one of the most famous and valuable books at that time. Then an old woman beggar, looking filthy and very thin, very undernourished, passed by him and said something like, "You are reading so passionately, but do you even understand a bit of it?" (Laughter)

Oh? Tiloba was very startled. Such an old, ugly beggar and dare talk like this in front of a pundit, a learned professor like me? He was kind of startled and didn't know how to react. Then the old beggar woman spit into his book and went away.

He was so angry because she dared to spit into this holy book. So he ran after her. But as he ran after her, she just murmured something in her throat and suddenly he cooled down, he didn't feel angry anymore. Then he stopped there, went back home, and started to think. Maybe he felt something was wrong about the way he was learning from the books.  So he thought, thought very hard.  He also thought very hard about why an old beggar woman would dare to spit into the holy book which all India has revered for thousands of years.

People even worshipped in front of the book, and offered money to the book.  They still do that nowadays in some of the countries, including India. I know, I've seen.  They just bow to the book, offer money and flowers to the book, and believe that's all there is to knowledge and wisdom.  But a book is a book.  You are you.  How can you bow to a book and get anything from it.  But many people believe it.

So this Tiloba thought very hard.  He was also surprised at how an old woman, so weak, could just murmur one or two sentences, and his anger which was like fire was put out as if by water.  So after sometime considering, he left his job, and didn't argue anymore.  He went all over to search for the old woman, the beggar, trying to find out what it was that he didn't understand.

One day he found her in a jungle alone.  He tried to argue with her, and use his eloquence and knowledge to beat her in the argument.  But it didn't matter how hard he tried, she always won.  The old, ugly, poor, undernourished beggar always won. (Master laughs.)  Finally she told him, "The things I know, the wisdom that I possess and understand is not in the books.  You cannot find it, therefore you can never win an arguement with me."

Finally he bowed to her, accepted her as a master, and asked her to teach him.  She did.  What she told him was that whatever you want to know is not in the books and it's not in this world.  You have to go and find heavenly beings to learn with.

So the way is initiation. We go up inside, then we find these heavenly beings.  That's what it means.  Then we learn with them.

Even if I teach you, even if any master teaches you, it's only verbally, only physically. If you want to learn something better, you have to go inside to a higher level of consciousness and learn with the inner master, the all pervading master, not the physical one. The physical one is only a ladder, to bring you up to higher stories of consciousness. There you learn with the higher master, even with the same master or with a different master, but at a higher, finer level of consciousness.

Afterward Tiloba forsook everything and tried hard to go to the heavenly realms, to meet these heavenly beings and study with them. The road to these heavenly beings is full of tricks, full of hardships, but he made it.

This was Tiloba. Even the greatest, knowledgeable man had to go and bow to an old, ugly, hungry, beggar woman for wisdom. So there is nothing too humble for us to go and bow for, to anyone who has wisdom, who can really show us the way to liberation.

Most of the masters of the old time were very poor. Jesus was a carpenter, he never had so much wealth. Buddha had a lot of wealth but he forsook it. (Master laughs.) So he also had nothing. He ran around India begging for food. He also became a beggar anyhow. Most of the masters don't possess anything. If they even want to do it, it's also fine.

One of the Sikh masters, the tenth Sikh master, he was very illustrious. He kept his wealth. He looked very wealthy, and he wore a lot of jewelry like a prince. He never shied away from that. But other Sikh masters go around the country begging for food also. So there is no need to say the master should be this, that or the other. No problem.

You see the Quan Yin Bodhisattva, she had a lot of ornaments, her hair was very long and beautiful, and she wore fine clothes. In heaven people are beautiful. Their ornaments are natural, attached to them according to their merit.

So there is no need to say the master always has to be poor. It is not necessarily so. Most of the masters, because of their inner realization, they choose the simple life. But the master always acts accordingly. It doesn't mean it always has to be like that; because if the master is so attached to poverty, to a simple life or to simple clothing alone, then it's also a kind of attachment. Always clinging to one thing or to another extreme, then it's also no good. The master must be detached inside, but outside it doesn't matter. It depends on your situation and your background, or whatever you have to do to benefit sentient beings.

# Impartial
## *Love*

Once there was a very small business-man who wasn't very well off. His business wasn't very successful, but he was all right. He was contented and took care of his family. There was another person, his neighbor, who was a practitioner of the Truth, and that man was very poor. So the businessman and neighbors gave him food and material aid from time to time, to see him through the winter and some of the hard times. Ever since he gave a little bit, very little, maybe one thousandth of his income — a little bread, sometimes cookies, a cabbage, a bunch of carrots, rice, things like that which didn't cost much — to his neighbor, the practitioner of the Truth, his business, his family and his health became better; his children became more obedient, things like that; and he earned more money.

So the more he earned, the more he gave to the practitioner next door, because now he had more money. The more he gave, the more he earned, the more his business boomed; and everything became better and better.

Then he began to associate his improvements with the charity that he gave to his neighbor, which was rightly so. He began to think to himself, "Ah, the more I give to this guy, the more my business will improve. Also, I heard that he has a master; and he told me his master is a million times greater than himself." Now, as a businessman, he thought, "Ah hah! Multi-million times more. If I give to just a lousy disciple and my business has already increased manifold, then if I give to his master who he says is a hundred, billion, million times better, greater than him, then my business..."

You can imagine what he was thinking to himself. (Everyone laughs.) So, he reached into his pocket and prepared a lot of precious gifts, money and everything; and went very far away to find the master of the neighbor.

Now, he went and made offerings to the master only, and didn't offer to the neighbor. Since he began making offerings to the greatest master that he had heard of, his business dwindled, just went down and down every day. The more he gave to the master, the less he got, until he could bear no more. He nearly went bankrupt, nearly had nothing in the house anymore, and all the family nearly died of starvation.

He went to the neighbor and talked to the so-called lousy disciple of the great master. He asked him, "How come you told me your master is multimillion times greater than you?"

The disciple said, "Yeah, of course, I told you the truth. My master is greater than I can describe. It's not a hundred million times better, greater. I cannot explain to you how great he is, so I just told you a hundred billion times better than me. But he's greater than that."

The businessman said, "But I went and made offerings to him because I thought he was greater, more distinguished, more virtuous and more worthy than you; and since then, my business has dwindled, I've nearly died of starvation, and the whole family has nothing to eat now. How come?"

The disciple said, "Ah, before you made offerings to me out of your good heart, your loving kindness. Because I was in need, you just gave to me without thinking of anything in return. You gave with love and with no expectations. You gave at random without thinking whether I was worthy or not, without choosing the recipient. You just gave because you loved.

"God also gives freely. Hes doesn't make distinctions between whom Hes gives, just like you did not make a distinction to whom you gave. You gave to me, you did not make distinctions whether I was good or bad, whether I was worthy or not. But since you made the distinction between me and my master – you chose the distinguished, the virtuous, the worthy, the highly respectable holy man – then you gave the charity because you thought he was worthy, he was distinguished and virtuous. God also did the same. Hes picked only the virtuous, the worthy and the holy to give to. Because you made a distinction, God also made a distinction."

So make sure that your love has no distinction when you go home. Your children may be very bad, your husband may be lousy, your neighbors may be very terrible, but try to love them. Not all the same love; but love accordingly, according to your own ability. Love as much as you can, and only when they need; then you help. If not, just treat them all equally, friendly and with a non-hatred quality in your heart; because you can't love everyone the same way.

God doesn't make us love everyone the same, so why should we? We don't have to force it; but we love them, meaning that whenever they need us, even if they have harmed us before, we turn around and help imme- diately. Loving them means that we don't harbor any hatred, ill- will or negative wish towards them; but wish them well, pray for them, meditate for them.

A **Thief**

Becomes A

**Spiritual**
**Practitioner**

Once when a thief tried to steal something in the palace, he overheard a conversation between two eunuchs: "Our king wants to marry the princess to a monk practicing on the banks of the Ganges River. What do you think about this?"

The other eunuch said, "Good! It is good! The princess is the most precious person in the country, and the monks practicing by the Ganges are also the most rare, most virtuous and most noble persons in the world. Naturally, I am delighted and agree with the idea!"

Hearing these words, the thief halted his stealing business, and stealthily went back to become a monk instead. (Laughter) Hastily he shaved his head and put on a monk's robe. Then he mixed among the monks to meditate, all the while hoping the princess would become his wife.

Several days later, the king really sent a eunuch to the banks of the Ganges River to ask the monks whether they would marry the princess. He asked one by one. Upon receiving a negative answer, he would ask the next one, and the next one.

The monks were good practitioners and didn't care about the princess, so all of them declined. Only the thief remained unasked, sitting there with his heart throbbing like mad. His mind screamed: "I am here! Come over quickly." (Laughter)

Finally, the eunuch went to ask him. When the eunuch asked him, he remained silent, (laughter) didn't say a word. All the others said they didn't want to, but he didn't say anything. It was already a great difference.

The eunuch was very happy, and reported to the king, "A monk practicing by the Ganges seems to have the intention of marrying the princess. We asked him, he didn't decline, which means he has consented ninety percent, only that he didn't decisively say he really agrees. Among those whom I asked, he was the only one who didn't say no."

Delighted by the good news, the king thought that he should go personally and take a lot of presents, then the monk would definitely agree to marry the princess.

The king took along all his counselors, generals and the eunuch, and went to the Ganges where the thief was meditating. With great respect, he asked the "monk" to marry the princess. As the king also practiced spiritually, he didn't want to marry the princess to an ordinary person. He preferred his daughter to marry a spiritual practitioner, so she could also practice in the company of a good husband, a good teacher. The king would only be satisfied having a son-in-law who could teach the princess how to meditate and to be a virtuous person. Therefore, upon hearing that a practitioner meditating by the Ganges would marry the princess, he was very happy. He showed him great respect, bowed to him, and asked him to marry his daughter.

The thief was complacent, but then he thought: "I have just shaved and put on a monk's robe, impersonating a monk, a spiritual practitioner, yet the king and all his counselors treat me with so much respect, and have offered me wealth and precious things. I can't imagine what it would be like if I were to become a real monk, a real spiritual practitioner!"

After consideration, he didn't want to marry the princess anymore! (Laughter) Instead, he started to practice seriously. Pretending in the first place, he now became a real monk because he perceived the benefits of spiritual practice. Since then, the thief meditated and practiced very sincerely. Eventually he was enlightened and became a great saint, a very famous spiritual practitioner.

# God

## Almighty Takes Care Of Everything

Once there was a very conscientious Indian yogi practitioner. One day his very old and sick mother died. He was very happy and immediately ran to the big hall. Kneeling there, he thanked God almighty, perhaps the inner Master! He prostrated and said, "Thank you God! I had not asked and had not prayed to You, but You have already given me a great blessing. Now that my mother has been taken away by You, I am very free and I'm able to think about You wholeheartedly every day without any encumbrance. Thank You!"

He was there joyously dancing and singing. The neighbors felt it very strange, "How come? His mother has died, he did not shed a tear, and he is even dancing and singing."

Meaning he was dancing a type of dance to make an offering to God, not that he was going to a karaoke; it was not the same! Perhaps it was about the same – moving and shaking – they looked the same. But his mother would not be sad because she was also a very pious spiritual practitioner, like himself. They both knew that the world is ephemeral. Thus his mother was very happy when she passed away, and he was also very happy after she passed away. They were both strange people!

After burying his mother, he went to the banks of the Ganges every day to recite the Holy Names, meditate, and communicate with God Almighty. It had been three days and this person had not eaten or drank anything. He totally forgot about it. He was sitting on one very secluded bank of the Ganges where no pilgrims pass by, thus he did not get anything to eat.

God Almighty spoke to the people beside Hirm, "Alas! What a pity! My disciple down there is dying of hunger and it seems as though I am not being very responsible, not giving him anything to eat. He is there, remembering me every minute of the day, yet I am here forgetting to protect him."

Then God told the angel beside Hirm to bring some good food to the riverside for him. A lot of blessed food was put on a gold plate – chapatis, milk, apples, et cetera, and brought to that person. That angel had never seen a human being before, not to mention a boy. Being a girl and a bit shy to see a boy, she silently put the plate beside him and flew away.

That person saw the food but did not see anyone come. He thanked God thinking it must have been sent by Hirm. He finished the food and continued to recite God's name, meditate, and enter samadhi. Suddenly a lot of people surrounded him and woke him up. They were carrying sticks and broad swords wanting to arrest him. Very puzzled he said, "Why? What is the matter?"

They said, "You thief. You dare to steal this gold plate from God's temple. We want to take you to the king to punish you."

No matter how he tried to explain, the soldiers would not believe him. They saw this poor boy in tattered clothes sitting by the river, and could not imagine that he could possess such a precious gold plate; thus they assumed that he must have stolen it. The plate looked like the ones used in the temple to make offerings to God, so they were taking him back to be punished.

After taking him back, the king was very angry. He told his subordinates to beat him. He was beaten for a long time, very hard and very seriously; but that yogi did not feel anything at all, just continued to laugh. (Master laughs.) Not laughing like I am, but about the same. He was not only laughing, he was also very happy like being tickled. They got tired of beating him; their hands were sore. (Master laughs.) Then they stopped beating him and let him go. The king also felt strange, as if God was protecting him; thus he dared not continue with the beating. But he was very curious and ran to the temple to see if such a plate had been stolen.

When he went to the temple, he saw blood flowing from God's statue. He was very surprised, "How could it be so? How could an idol bleed?"

Not only that, the places that were bleeding were exactly the places as on that person which had been beaten. Therefore, he knelt there repenting, not knowing what sins he had committed. Later he realized that perhaps that person was innocent, beating him was like beating God; thus God's statue was bleeding.

At that point, the king and his ministers were all very frightened. They all hurried to the riverside, knelt, and repented to that small, penniless yogi; they also began to offer him food every day. When they went back to the temple, they saw that God's statue was no longer bleeding. Hence, they knew the reason.

Because this person was very earnest in his meditation — he thought only about God every day—God felt guilty because he did not have anything to eat. If it was because of the food that he was beaten, then of course it was God's fault. Thus Hes bore the punishment Hirmself. It is not that after being God or Buddha you care about nothing. If we truly practice sincerely then God will take care of everything.

# Secret Way

## To
## Achieve Immortality

**O**nce upon a time, there was a person in China who often told people that he knew a secret way to achieve immortality. The emperor of Yan State sent his attendant and chancellor to look for this person who knew about immortality, to bring him to the royal court so as to learn his secret way. However, that attendant was much like our Quan Yin messengers here, or my attendant! He went very slowly. Instead of driving a Mercedes Benz or a Buick, he drove an Yu Long, so he went very slowly. Oh! He was not driving an Yu Long even, he drove a horse-drawn carriage. Thinking that was too luxurious, he rode a horse. Later, he thought even a horse was too much, so he simply went on foot! It was so slow, so slow!

He enjoyed all kinds of pleasures throughout his journey, and was sidetracked to Paris and many places. Therefore, he took a long time to reach the place of the man who knew the secret way to achieve immortality. Because he was too slow and too late, the man had already died. (Laughter)

The emperor of Yan State was furious. You know, it was just like when I roar, but he wasn't as good because he didn't practice the Quan Yin Method. (Laughter) He didn't roar as loud because I have the chi through practicing the Quan Yin Method. I can roar much louder than he did. It is great fun to be angry this way. (Laughter)

The emperor was so angry that he wanted to execute the attendant. Then, a chancellor begged the emperor to forgive the attendant and spare his life. He said to the emperor, "In this world, all human beings strive to live, and fear death. If we kill this person because of a way to achieve immortality, this is against our ideal. Besides, the person who boasted that he knew the secret of immortality is dead. He could not save himself. That means his secret was useless! Therefore, please do not kill our useful person for a useless man."

The emperor of Yan State felt that his words were reasonable, so he started to chant the Holy Names, observe the Five Precepts, and followed Suma Ching Hai's principal of not killing! (Laughter)

At that time, there was another state called Qi.    There, a person named Hutzu had also heard about the man who knew the secret way to achieve immortality, which he was also keen to learn.    When he knew about the death of this man, he was extremely frustrated, and cried sadly.   His friend Futzu laughed loudly and said, "You stupid fool!   That man said he knew the secret of immortality, yet he is dead now.    Can't you see that he was actually a fool? What are you crying for?   This shows that you have no wisdom, and have no idea about what you want to learn."

Hutzu retorted to his friend Futzu, "You are very wrong! Some people know some secret ways, but because they do not know how to use them, they cannot use them.    There are also some people who know how to use the secret ways, but they do not know where the true method is being imparted.

"For instance, previously in Wei State, there was a person who was an expert mathematician.   Before he died, he imparted all his calculation methods to his son.   This son heard everything, but he couldn't calculate as well as his father.   A person from another place came to this son and asked to learn the calculation methods.   When he went home, he could calculate and solve any mathematical problem accurately, exactly like the father.   He simply acted according to the words of the son, who didn't know about mathematics, and practiced them step by step. As a result, he did it as well as the deceased father.

"The man who knew the secret way to achieve immortality might have known the method himself, but he didn't use it or practice it accordingly.   It would have been wonderful if we could have learned the secret way from him, and practiced it ourselves!"

So it is with the Quan Yin Method. Observing that you can sit for such a long time – sit for ten hours without moving – and have such good experiences, it shows that this method is the right one. This secret method is orthodox. So, if you can carry on practicing by following Master's instructions, you cannot go wrong! Sometimes, I send Quan Yin messengers to teach you, then you practice by following the verbal instructions of the Quan Yin messenger. It does not matter if I am not there. Just follow the method to meditate, and you can have very good experiences.

The Quan Yin messengers may not be superior to you in spiritual practice, so you don't have to worship them. Worship your original nature instead. Worship the almighty Master power within, which is originally latent in us. Through the Quan Yin messengers and proper practice of the method taught by Master, we can definitely attain the Tao that we aspire for. However, though we say it this way, the method is not the most important! Our inner power can only be activated when live energy is transmitted into us.

The truth is, this person just happened to know this secret method; perhaps he learned it from a master who had attained the Truth. Therefore, it is all right for another person to learn from him. These secret methods are not to be found everywhere. Why did no one else, except that old man in Yan State, know about the secret of achieving immortality? And, why did he die despite his knowing it?

There are two explanations. First, perhaps the people of Yan and Qi States misunderstood his words about immortality. Immortality doesn't mean that our physical bodies will exist forever, but that our souls will be liberated in eternity. When we have attained the state of no birth and no death, no destruction and no

creation, no contamination and no purity, then we are really im-
mortal. However, when ordinary human beings hear about immortality, they think of the material aspect. Therefore, they were
disappointed upon knowing about the death of that person, or
they laughed at others for trying to learn immortality from him: "If
the teacher himself died, why are you learning from him?" I think
this is a more accurate explanation.

Another explanation is: Perhaps that person had learned
the secret method, but he didn't practice it. Perhaps, there really
was a way for people to live without getting old, live for several
thousand years, or tens of thousands of years. We should not
jump to conclusions about what exists and what does not. Before
we really know, don't deny anything. Should we really not know,
then we say we don't know. If we know, then we say: "Yes, I
know."

If that person knew the way to achieve immortality, then
why did he have to die? Perhaps because he didn't continue to
practice according to the method his master taught him, or he
didn't practice this method seriously, so he didn't have any result.
This is also very possible.

For instance, many people know how to practice Tai Chi
Chuan, or how to dance tango, rumba or cha cha, which they can
learn from books. The first step is with the right foot, the second
one is with the left, turn left, and then right, forward, backwards
and so on. He knows it all, he has the illustrations of the dance
steps. However, he does not practice them; or he practiced for
only a day or two, and doesn't go to the club frequently to dance,
so he forgets.

If we obtain these illustrations from him, we can practice
them. Perhaps it is not really perfect; but once we learn the basic

steps, we can practice and get better.  Maybe we can practice with an expert, then we will improve further. Later, adding our intelligent personality, and demonstrating our talent, we can dance even more beautifully.

Why, during that time in China, only that person was known to know the secret way to achieve immortality, and no one else knew the same method?   Perhaps it is just like our Quan Yin messengers, not every place can have several of them.   For instance, there are only one or two masters, not many of their disciples are capable of transmitting the method, and it is not always possible to send dozens of them to each place.   This is why, at that time, in that country, people heard that only that person knew. (Applause)

# The Trap Of Giving

## Giving

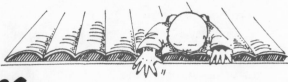

# Charity

**T**his is a story of bhiksuni Sukla.

One day the Lord of the Worlds, the Buddha was residing at the Jetavana Ashram during the Sarasvati period. He gave a lecture on the dharma to the four devotee groups (meaning the male and female devotees, both monastic and lay). At that time, there was a very rich elder who had a very beautiful daughter. There was one thing very special about this girl. She was wrapped in a piece of white cloth when she was born. Her parents were bewildered so they sought advice from a fortune-teller. The fortune-teller said, "You do not have to worry. This girl is abundant in blessed merits. I name her Sukla."

As the girl grew up, the piece of cloth on her body grew with her. She also became very pretty and elegant. Being a girl from a good family with a nice background, a lot of people came to propose marriage. However, she was not interested in anyone.

One day, her father summoned some very skillful craftsmen to make some beautiful adornments for her so-called trousseau. She asked her father, "What are all these ornaments for?"

Her father said, "You are an adult now, I should prepare for your marriage!"

The daughter told her father, "Marriage only lasts for a short time span. It is not of much use and can even create a lot of distress for us. I do not want to be married. I want to become a nun. It is much better to become a nun and get liberation."

She was the only child of her parents. Since they could not dissuade her, they did not insist anymore and agreed to let her become a nun. The next day, the father went out to buy some cloth. He wanted to have some monastic clothes made for her. The daughter asked, "I am going to become a nun, why are you still preparing all these clothes?"

Her father said, "I am going to make you some nun's robes."

The daughter shook her head and said, "It is not necessary. It is enough that I have this piece of cloth on my body."

Her parents were bewildered and did not know what to say, so they brought her to visit the Buddha. Of course, Sukla begged the Buddha to let her shave her head and devote monastically. She said to the Buddha, "My honorable Lord of the Worlds, it is difficult to secure a human body, to hear about the dharma, and to meet a living Buddha. Now that I have a human body, have heard about the dharma, and met the Buddha, please, my merciful Lord, let me shave, devote monastically, and be liberated from the transmigration of birth and death... et cetera."

What did the Buddha say then? "Very well bhiksu."

As He finished speaking, her hair suddenly dropped off (Master and everyone laugh), and the piece of cloth on her body also turned into a robe. Well! That was really convenient! In this way, we could save on the razor and blades, save on the clothing and everything. (Everyone laughs.) After that, Buddha handed her over to bhiksuni Mahaprajapati as a student – to teach her the dharma. She was very diligent in practicing and attained arhatship very soon.

Ananda was very curious so he closed his palms, knelt down, and asked Buddha, "My honorable Lord of the Worlds, what merits did bhiksuni Sukla attain in her past life that enabled her to be born wrapped in a cloth and into a noble family, as well as attain arhatship so soon after she had devoted monastically? Would my Lord please tell us so we can understand?"

180

The Buddha told Ananda that long ago there was a Buddha who descended to this world. His name was Vipasyin. He was always going about with his disciples to deliver sentient beings. Everywhere, kings, officials and citizens respected him very much. They gave him offerings, and organized many big spiritual gatherings for the Buddha, requesting him to give lectures on the dharma.

At that time, there was a very broad-minded bhiksu who liked to make affinities with people. Therefore every day, he went out to beg for food from every house and family, giving them blessed rewards in return. He also preached and introduced the true dharma of Ju-lai (the ultimate enlightenment) to everyone.

There was a young woman whose family was extremely poor. She and her husband had only one piece of cloth for the two of them to cover their bodies. If her husband was going out to beg, then she would give him that cloth while she would have nothing to wear at home. If it was the wife's turn to go out to beg, then the husband would stay at home, sitting and waiting on some hay.

One day, the bhiksu passed by their house on his way begging. He saw the young woman and said to her, "Oh young lady! You should realize that it is difficult to get a human body, to hear about the dharma, and to meet a Buddha... Now there is a living Buddha in this world who always preaches the dharma and scriptures. You should go there and listen to the dharma, then you will surely achieve infinite merits. You are now destitute. Because you were mean and stingy and didn't give any alms before, therefore you are getting this retribution now. If you give alms in this lifetime, you will definitely get a wealthy retribution in the future."

The young woman was very delighted upon hearing this. She asked the bhiksu to wait outside while she went inside and spoke to her husband, "Look at the sramana (meaning bhiksu) outside. He has come to advise us to go and see a living Buddha and to listen to his preaching. He has also advised us to give alms in order to get a wealthy retribution. He said our poverty in this life is the result of our failing to give alms and our endless greed in our past lives. Now we must sow some seeds of goodness so we can expect to live better in our next life."

After listening to her, her husband said, "What are we to do! We haven't anything in our home. We do not even know whether we will have anything to eat tomorrow. What alms could we possibly give?"

However, the woman insisted by saying, "Since I have already decided to give, I must give! If we do not give this time, we will come back in our next life and live as pitifully as we are now, or even worse."

Her husband was thinking, "Oh! Maybe my wife has secretly hidden some property and did not tell me!" So he said to his wife, "Well! If you really want to give, then give as you wish."

His wife said, "Alright! Since you have agreed, I will take this piece of cloth, our only possession, and offer it to that bhiksu. Please give it to me quickly!"

At that time, her husband began to show some concern and said, "Oh, no! The two of us depend on this piece of cloth in order to go out to beg. What shall we do from now on if you offer it to the bhiksu?  Are we going to sit here and starve to death?"

His wife then told him, "My husband, we will die sooner or later, no matter if we give alms or not.  So why don't we give now, so that even after we die, there is still a little blessed reward saved for our future?"

This husband thought that his wife sounded very reasonable so he finally agreed, "You just offer that piece of cloth to him and it will be good."

Before the wife took the cloth outside for the offering, she asked the bhiksu to climb onto the roof of the house.  It would be quite shameful to be seen without any clothes after she had made the offering.  She said, "My virtuous one, would you please climb onto the roof of the house?  I have one thing to offer you."

The bhiksu was very bewildered, "If you are going to offer me something, then do it here.  Why do you ask me to go up to the roof?"

The woman said, "Please understand, my virtuous one.  My husband and I have only this one piece of cloth which we are going to offer to you.  After we give it to you, it would be very impolite for us to face you without any clothing.  If you are on the roof while I am hiding in the house, then you would not be offended when you come down after the offering."

The bhiksu went up onto the roof while the woman went inside the house and locked the door.  She then opened the window and threw the piece of cloth up to the roof as an offering to him.  He appreciated and accepted the sincere offering of the couple, even though the cloth was dirty, worn-out and worthless.  He then blessed the couple, and took the cloth back as an offering to the Buddha.

As soon as he came back to the place where Vipasyin Buddha was, the Buddha asked him immediately, "Bhiksu, give me that piece of cloth."

The bhiksu realized that the Buddha knew about it so he said, "Would the Buddha please accept the sincerity of this couple?"

After Vipasyin Buddha received the cloth, he looked at it so tenderly. At that time, he was preaching to a large congregation which included the king, chancellors, soldiers, some rich noblemen and the general public. Everyone was respectfully and attentively listening to the Buddha's talk. Suddenly they saw the Buddha holding a piece of cloth which was old, worn-out and dirty, kind of like a wiping cloth; and he kept staring at it. Everyone felt very strange and were greatly surprised. The Buddha read everyone's mind so he told them, "Of all the alms-giving persons in this congregation, I can find no one who can surpass the person who has just offered me this piece of cloth."

Upon hearing the statement of the Buddha, everyone was startled. The queen immediately took off all the clothing on her body including her adornments and jewelry, et cetera. Then the king also took off all his clothing and gave all the money he was carrying, including the money of his retinue. He then sent someone with all of these things to invite the poor couple to accept their offerings and join their

congregation. As they knew that the couple had nothing to wear, they therefore took off all of their clothing for them. At that moment, Vipasyin Buddha took this opportunity to expound upon the merits of charity for everyone, so as to warn everyone about the quality of miserliness and the retribution of greed.

Shakyamuni Buddha reminded Ananda, "Ananda, you should realize that the destitute woman is the bhiksuni Sukla now. Because of her sincere, pure offering, no matter where she was born in the following ninety-one aeons, she always had a piece of cloth wrapped around her body. She also always had a wealthy, comfortable and peaceful life. She was able to meet me and attained arhatship because she had listened to the preaching of a living Buddha and resolved to achieve liberation. You people should also take this as an example to practice diligently and be eager to give alms."

After this lecture by the Buddha, many people resolved to make offerings and give alms. Everyone was satisfied and filled with the joy of the dharma.

Do you have any doubts, opinions or comments about this story? Have you resolved to give or offer anything? In that congregation, everyone decided to give alms so that they could all attained arhatship! Don't you feel strange about this piece of cloth? This piece of cloth actually belonged to the two of them, is that right? It just happened that she requested it for the offering. In this way she got the cloth for ninety-one aeons. By offering a dirty, worn-out, old cloth, she got a white cloth in return and later even attained arhatship. This is really incredible.

Since the cloth belonged to both the husband and wife, then why did only the wife receive the blessed rewards? We did not hear that the husband had received any benefits. It was because the wife initiated the offering while her husband originally did not want to offer. He only changed his mind later! His willingness was a little slow. (Everyone laughs.) So if you want to do anything, you had better decide quickly and do it fast, in order to get the best prize.

Just by offering sincerely to the disciple of a living Buddha, she was wrapped each time with that white cloth for ninety-one aeons (an aeon of time can be equal to billions of years), and was always born into a wealthy family. Finally she met a living Buddha and attained arhatship, so fast that even Ananda could not match her. Ananda attained arhatship only after Shakyamuni Buddha was gone, while this bhiksuni succeeded within a few short months after initiation.

However, do you think that it is good to give alms? (Audience: It's not the ultimate.) Not the ultimate! Transmigrating between life and death for ninety-one aeons of time just for that piece of cloth, that's really terrible! Actually, if she had not given alms at that time and asked for liberation instead, then she would have been liberated in one life. She would not need all those merits later on. Unfortunately she did not ask for ultimate liberation when she was giving alms. She gave because she wanted a wealthier life in the future.

Whose fault was that? Was it her own fault? No! It was the fault of the bhiksu, the Buddha's disciple. He did not tell her about the supreme method. He just introduced to her the merits within the three realms. He just said that if you give alms, you can get merits in return; thus enhancing the greed within them. If he had told the woman, "You may be poor now, but never mind. There is a living Buddha on Earth. If you follow him to practice and resolve to achieve liberation, the heavenly kingdom is fully loaded with all kinds of treasures. You can get whatever you want after liberation. No matter how rich you are, as long as you are in this world, it will not be better than in heaven, nor greater than nirvana."

Wouldn't it have been better if he had said it this way? This is why Master does not emphasize charity, fearing that the greed for wealth would arise within you. Wherever I go, I would not stress charity. Even if I did, I would have included — tolerance against insult, diligence, samadhi and wisdom. I would say that it is only one part of the whole and not important. I have always told you that charity is nothing great, because we came with nothing and will later leave with nothing. We owe this world a lot. Even when we give a little to some other people, it is just to repay our debts. You cannot really count this as charity.

Therefore, we can tell from here the difference between the supreme method and an ordinary method. An ordinary method would advise people to be charitable for future merits in return... et cetera, and then slowly, slowly advance towards nirvana. Ninety-one aeons! Amitabha! Do you know how long ninety-one aeons is? We could not even bear ninety-one lifetimes, let alone ninety-one aeons.

Everytime you are born you have to experience birth, aging, illness and death, no matter how rich you are. We are in pain each time we are born, when we get old, when we are ill, and in even more pain when we experience death and separation. Then between your birth and death there is still a lot of injustice, a lot of severe or lighter suffering, a lot of unexpected emotions and adverse encounters. It is really not worthwhile to live for ninety-one aeons in this way.

If the wisdom in your mind does not emerge, and does not think in the direction of the ultimate liberation, then there is no use in whatever you are practicing. What good is there if you are just wandering around within the three realms!? It is the same even for a king — the same experiences of birth, aging, illness and death; the same headaches and a heap of worldly distresses. Therefore you should understand that the supreme method is different from those ordinary methods within the three realms. Whatever objective we have in our mind, we will achieve that objective. Whatever we really want in our heart, our soul, our wisdom we'll sooner or later acquire it for ourselves.

When that poor woman made the offering, she had not seen the Buddha. She just heard the bhiksu say that alms giving would bring her a wealthy retribution. A better alternative was not presented to her. She heard this statement about alms giving and wealthy retributions from a bhiksu, so she thought that it was good and must be the truth. Therefore, she believed him immediately and pledged such a wish. You must realize that she was concentrating all of her energies, her thoughts, speech and actions into her wish at that moment. Therefore she had to come back to enjoy her blessed reward for ninety-one aeons.

This statement was made by a bhiksu with sound practice and merits. Therefore his statement was powerful and capable of creating an impact. It was the first time that woman heard about such good things. She had been in pain all of her life. Now that there was such a good way to relieve the suffering of her future life, of course she would put all her body and mind into wishing for that.

You cannot always focus all your actions, speech and thoughts on one thing, unless you are a great practitioner. Otherwise, you will exhaust all your energy on the wish you made. Even if she happened to see the Buddha, it would have already been too late. All her energies had been exhausted on her previous wish for blessed rewards in her next life. Therefore, she had to remain there for ninety-one aeons to enjoy that wish. Fortunately, she did see the Buddha and was awakened a little. However, she had very little

vitality left at that time so she had to incarnate for ninety-one aeons. So you see how we could harm people like this?

It is said in the Buddhist scriptures that the person who makes the offering must be pure in their intent, feel happy, and be desireless in their giving. The one who accepts the offering should be the same – desireless, feel happy to receive, and be pure. In this way, the two of them can receive blessed rewards. Both the person who makes the offering and the one who takes the offering should be like this. No wonder that woman had to incarnate for ninety-one aeons before she could attain arhatship. It is terrible to have to wait for ninty-one aeons in order to get liberation! Ninety-one ae-ons almost means that you do not have to practice anymore.

Actually she had not received any blessed rewards at all. She had already met the Buddha, yet she had to wait for ninety-one aeons before she could be liberated. You can get liberation as soon as you meet a Buddha, in one lifetime. The problem was that she ran into the Buddha's disciple first, then concentrated all her ener-gies on that wish, not knowing that there was a better way.

Therefore when you go out to preach to other people, do not talk about those worthless things, do not provoke their greed or their material desires within the three realms. You should persuade them to aim for liberation right away. Never mind if he

does not listen. He can always earn other merits and blessed rewards from other places and methods introduced by other people. We should not advise people to do those worthless things.

"Seek you first the Kingdom of God and all other things shall be added unto you." This is really the case. If not, what is the use in advising people to perform those small deeds and get those tiny blessed rewards in return? It is simply a hindrance to other people. So, if there is someone who advises others to give offerings for future merits in other lifetimes, these people are really doing incredibly great harm to others. Yet they are so proud and self-flattered, thinking that they are really great.

This is really horrible. They have created karma which they are not aware of, and are still flattering themselves about it. If he himself gives offerings and then enjoys the transmigration of life and death for ninety-one aeons all by himself, we have nothing to say. However, if he leads all people, millions or billions of them to do the same thing for fame, benefits and the blessed rewards in their future lives, it is really too horrible. The most dreadful thing is that they obstruct people from attaining liberation.

The most important thing in spiritual practice is to attain a correct concept and a proper method. After that, it would be good enough for us to live a perfectly ordinary life. Incorrect concepts and improper methods bring about troubles.

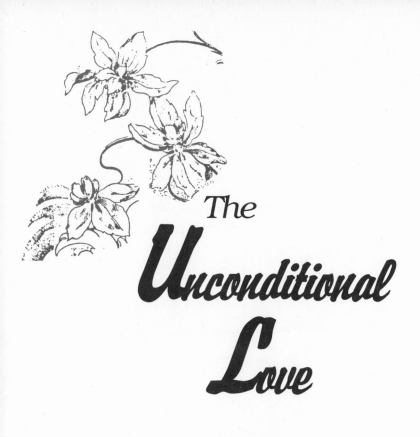

# The
# *Unconditional*
# *Love*
## Of The Master

THE MARKET PLACE

There was an enlightened master in America whose name was Yogananda. He first met his master on a street in the market before he was initiated by this master. He had great faith in this master, so he asked to learn the method. The master consented and said, "Come to me another day, then I will give you the initiation and take you as my disciple." He instructed Yogananda further, "Today, I have come looking for you. However, when you go to my place, it will be you looking for me. You have to beseech me then. You cannot just casually come and ask me to give you the initiation."

Yogananda said, "No problem, I will do as you say."

Later, he went and asked the master to impart the method

to him.

Do you know why they had to behave like this? The formality was still necessary to check whether he cherished the method or not. The master feared that he might take him just as his friend, since they had already met. Then he would just go in and say, "Hi! Will you impart the method to me? We met each other in the marketplace when we bought the same sort of vegetables. Do you remember me?" (Laughter)

It was possible that Yogananda would go to him with this attitude, so he said, "When you come to me, you must behave solemnly and seriously, and bow down begging me to accept you. Only then will I transmit the method to you. Though we have already understood each other today, you still have to bow when you come to me."

The first reason was formality. The second reason was to determine his humility. The third reason was to keep a distance of respect between the master and disciple. There were many disciples looking at them. If he treated a particular disciple too casually, it would be difficult for him to teach other disciples afterwards. Besides, being a newcomer who didn't know the rules, he might be too hot-headed and say, "We bought vegetables together that day, and you promised to impart the method to me. What actually is this method? Will you take it out and show it to me?" (Laughter)

So, he had to give him clear instructions. He was a truly compassionate master. In addition to transmitting the method to him, he also taught him the proper behavior for a disciple.

That day, Yogananda went to his master's place, beseeched him, and completed all formalities. Before he was taught the method, his master told him, "Unconditionally, I take you as my disciple. Regardless of how high or low your spiritual level or morality is, how good or bad your personality is, and how noble or awful your behavior is, I will forever love you, protect you, and accept you as my best friend."

Yogananda said, "Okay!"

Of course it was really nice having such a master!

His master continued to say seriously, "However, I have one condition."

His heart skipped a beat. Suddenly there was a condition.

His master said, "My only condition is that, in the same way I accept you, you should also accept and love me unconditionally. You have to love me regardless of my level, my mood or how good or bad my behavior is. Can you do it?"

Yogananda hesitated and said, "Master, being an enlightened master, of course your level is very high. We adore you because you are supreme. As you just said, you might be very low sometimes; but if I feel that you are acting wrongly, immorally or very low spiritually, I may not be able to accept it." (Laughter)

Then, his master said, "Alright! I don't need your friendship. It stinks!"

He meant he was a terrible friend, and this kind of friend was not a real friend.

Much ashamed, Yogananda said, "I am sorry master. I will always love you, regardless of your level, your morality and your mood. Even if you fall, I will protect you."

His master was delighted and said, "This is good! Okay, I will accept you as my disciple."

Then he initiated Yogananda.

Why did his master make such a request? Did he need his faithful heart? I also don't know why he asked him this? I have never asked you to do this. It's not that he is imperfect, but that he feared his disciple would judge him with the mind and ability of an ordinary human. So he strengthened his faith in advance. Therefore, he said, "No matter what will become of me, you still have to love and respect me."

This would keep him from incurring karma and from having his faith shaken. Since he had promised, he ought to keep his word.

Hence, whenever he observed something wrong with the behavior of his master, he would remember that moment and he wouldn't make casual remarks. He would also remember that his master accepted him. If the master can accept us, why can't we accept the master?

If we believe our master is enlightened, he will be able to see our karma, our virtues and faults. He can observe them very clearly, yet he still accepts us as his disciples. He still loves us and saves us whenever we fall. Being ordinary humans, we cannot see karma, virtues and faults, so how can we just criticize him like that? The master demands this of us only because he wants to strengthen our faith, and keep us from incurring karma. It's not that the enlightened master is imperfect, he is a most perfect being. If he were not perfect, he could not be omnipresent, and he could not save his disciples with his innumerable manifestation bodies, neither could he listen and respond to the whole universe.

Sometimes, we may not have many experiences, but other fellow practitioners have, so our faith is also affirmed. If a person can always hear and respond to every other person, there must be something great about him. Besides, all his contributions and help are rendered unconditionally. Therefore, we will have faith though we don't have many experiences. In case you still have no faith after listening to those stories, God will go to hell to save you, no one else. Therefore, when we read these stories, don't just turn the pages, learn from them!

Suppose our master is not perfect, then how about us? Are we perfect? Are we justified in criticizing him? No? Then forget it! Therefore, it is not difficult to pursue spiritual practice, but difficult to keep our faith. The more we think we have very strong faith, the more tests will come to us. We will encounter few tests if we don't think that we are great and merciful, very firm in faith, and if we are not eager to deliver sentient beings. Being an ordinary human, the Maya power won't bother us because we have no great expectations.

If we want to deliver sentient beings, we need to have great power and attain Buddhahood quickly, preferably yesterday. (Master and everyone laugh.) But then, do not complain when tests befall you. If you don't want to have so many tests, don't expect too much. See what we can do within our capacity, what we did in the past, and what we can do in the future.

It is very helpful to have faith, but not everyone can maintain it. I am not blaming anyone, but we should know our weaknesses, and prepare mentally. When we fall to a certain level and lose faith, we will remember that the master once told us that we are very weak and feeble sentient beings who cannot withstand the slightest affliction. You have read many stories, and you know it is very difficult to keep your faith.

It is easier for us to worship a wooden Buddha than a living one. The living Buddha has to handle innumerable situations and jobs, and in many different ways. When we observe that his ways of doing things are not up to our taste — our "noble" taste, "enlightened" taste — we think the Buddha is bad. We cannot understand, so we guess blindly.

That enlightened master didn't mind whether his disciples doubted him or not, he just wanted to teach his disciples how to protect their faith.

One day, Yogananda ran away. Why did he run away? It was because he had stayed with his master for a long time, but he didn't seem to have any "experiences"! He heard that there were great spiritual masters practicing in some mountain caves at a certain place. So he went to the Ganges and climbed the mountains to find and to live with them for some days. However, all the enlightened masters there told him that he had already found the right master, and that he should go back. He also had some very good experiences there. This was one of his stories.

Once he went to a mountain cave because he heard there was a great saint there, a senior fellow brother of his master, related to his master's lineage. He heard that this practitioner was great – probably "greater" than his master, because he was senior to him. He climbed mountains, crossed

rivers, and found the cave. There he sat with great expectations in his heart, humbly massaging the master's feet to get blessings.

At night, he found that the whole place was very bright. It was bright regardless of whether his eyes were open or closed, so he couldn't sleep. He asked, "Master, why is it like this? You have no lamps here, and there is no lighting outside. Why is the place so bright?"

The enlightened master told him, "Go to sleep! Don't ask so many questions!"

He laid down, but he couldn't sleep. Again he complained, "How can I get to sleep? It is so bright no matter whether my eyes are closed or not!"

Then the enlightened master said, "All right, since you cannot go to sleep, let us get up and have some tea."

They had tea together and chatted until daybreak. Then the master in the cave told him, "Go back! Go back to your master. You have found the right one, don't wander around anymore."

He was very ashamed. He believed the words of this senior brother of his master.

When he went back to his master's place, he sneaked into the kitchen; but his master was already there waiting for him. He didn't blame him at all. He just said, "Hey! Have you eaten? Come! I'll cook something for you."

They had a meal together. After they finished the meal, his master said, "We have to cook more. Later, at two o'clock in the morning, a large group of people will come from faraway to see me, and they will be very hungry."

Yogananda wondered, "It is strange! How could the master know about this when he was here? Perhaps he is really great. Otherwise, how could he know these things?"

There was no telephone and no messenger had come, but his master just knew it naturally. Yogananda was doubtful, but his master wouldn't joke about this kind of thing. He helped his master prepare the meal and got ready to serve it. Later, at two o'clock, many people really did come, and they ate.

After finishing the cooking, his master left to take a rest. Later, he took Yogananda to a place outside a door. When they sat down, his master patted him on his chest. Then he had a sensational inner experience. In his vision, he saw that everything looked different, very transparent and very bright. His body seemed nonexistent, and the whole world became transparent. Everything was very bright and looked different. He was extremely grateful to his master, so he knelt, then prostrated to him.

His master shook his head and said, "Poor boy! What can mountains and rivers give you?"

Yogananda had just been on a pilgrimage to the mountains and rivers, so he understood. From then on, he never left his master again.

# Introduction Of Our Publications

## (1) The Key Of Immediate Enlightenment

Au Lac and Chinese editions: Books 1-8
Thai edition: Books 1-6
English edition: Books 1-5
Korean edition: Books 1-4
Spanish edition: Books 1-3
German, Portugese and Indonesian editions: Books 1 & 2
French, Japanese, Polish, Swedish and Hungarian editions:
Book 1

## (2) The Key Of Immediate Enlightenment
### *Questions and Answers*

Au Lac edition: Books 1-4
Chinese, Indonesian and Korean editions: Books 1 & 2
English, Portugese, Polish, French, Hungarian and
German editions: Book 1

## (3) The Key Of Immediate Enlightenment
### *Correspondences Between Master and Disciples*

Chinese and Au Lac editions: Books 1 & 2
Spanish edition: Book 1

## (4) The Key Of Immediate Enlightenment
### *My Wondrous Experiences With Master*

Chinese and Au Lac editions: Books 1 & 2

## (5) The Key Of Immediate Enlightenment
### *Special Edition*

Seven-Day Retreat in San Di Mun in 1992
English edition: Book 1

## (6) Silent Tears
Chinese, English and Au Lac in one edition: Book 1
English, French and German in one edition: Book 1
Spanish edition, Portuguese edition, Philippino edition and
Korean edition: Book 1

## (7) Aphorisms
Spanish and Korean editions: Book 1
Chinese and English in one edition: Book 1
German and French in one edition: Book 1

## (8) Collection Of Art Creations By Suma Ching Hai
Chinese, English and Au Lacese in one edition

## (9) "Supreme Kitchen" International Vegetarian Cuisine
English and Chinese in one edition: Books 1 & 2

## (10) I Have Come To Take You Home
English edition: Book 1

## (11) Master Tells Stories
English edition: Book 1

*Cassettes and videotapes of lectures in Chinese, English, Au Lac, Spanish, Portuguese, Indonesian, Thai, Japanese, Korean, French, German, Cantonese etc. are available. Detailed catalogue will be sent on request. Direct inquiries are welcome.*

Information concerning the Quan Yin Method can be obtained
from the following sites:
World-Wide-Web host servers (WWW)
http://fiber.ieo.nctu.edu.tw:5000/ (host in Formosa)
http://quanyin.org (host in U.S.A)
http://www.magi.com/~quanyin/homepage.html (host in Canada)
http://www.chinghai.com (host in Singapore)
*On the WWW, there are three languages - Chinese, English and Au Lac,
and five different codes.

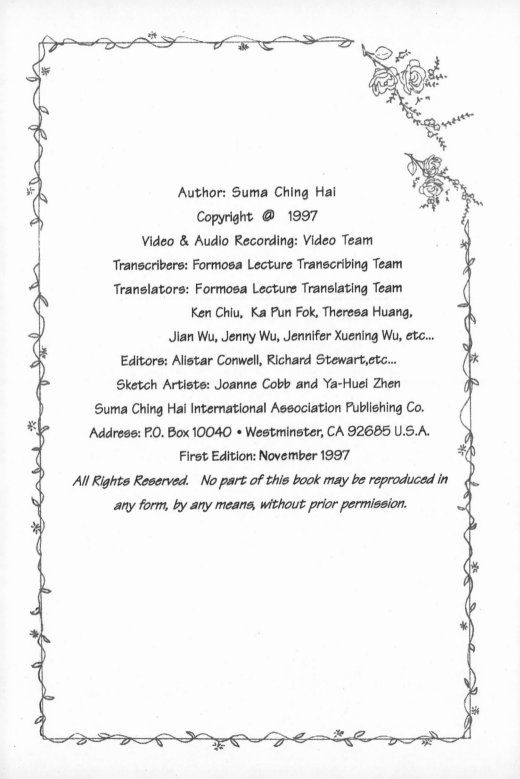

Author: Suma Ching Hai

Copyright @ 1997

Video & Audio Recording: Video Team

Transcribers: Formosa Lecture Transcribing Team

Translators: Formosa Lecture Translating Team

Ken Chiu, Ka Pun Fok, Theresa Huang,

Jian Wu, Jenny Wu, Jennifer Xuening Wu, etc...

Editors: Alistar Conwell, Richard Stewart,etc...

Sketch Artists: Joanne Cobb and Ya-Huei Zhen

Suma Ching Hai International Association Publishing Co.

Address: P.O. Box 10040 • Westminster, CA 92685 U.S.A.

First Edition: November 1997